A STUDY ON
THE PURE THEORY OF
PRODUCTION

A STUDY ON
THE PURE THEORY OF
PRODUCTION

BY

SUNE CARLSON

KELLEY & MILLMAN, INC.

NEW YORK

1956

Printed in U.S.A.

———

Noble Offset Printers, Inc.
New York 3, N. Y.

PREFACE

While working on this essay I have often felt like a composer who writes a rhapsody on old folk tunes. The main theme has been clear to me from the beginning; it is nothing but the folk tune of all economists, that a firm should so plan its production that the discounted marginal cost of its output is equal to the discounted marginal revenue and every productive service is employed until its discounted marginal value productivity equals its discounted marginal cost. My contribution, therefore, is not one of melody but of arrangement, (mathematical) orchestration and variation. In the first part of the essay the familiar theme is gradually built up against the simplest setting: a single firm produces a single commodity in a single "closed" time period; not until the fourth chapter is the theme developed in full. The fifth and sixth chapters are variations upon the preceding motif: but the setting is less restricted; more variables are allowed to play. Even when I discuss "joint" production and "capitalistic" or, as I have preferred to call it, "poly-periodic" production, the analysis ends upon the same well-known melody.

Although economists have long recognized the main relationships of the theory of production, these relationships have not been co-ordinated in a single body of theory — except in such works as those of Frisch and Schneider — but have been scattered in isolated fragments throughout cost theory, capital and interest theory and the theory of distribution. To bring together and co-ordinate in one consistent scheme the different relationships of the theory of production has been the main purpose of this essay. I have tried particularly to emphasize the bearing of the capital and interest theory on the cost and revenue calculations of a single firm's production. But while my main purpose has been the co-ordination of relationships already known, I have also tried to develop the old relationships in new directions. So, for instance, I have discussed the technical and cost relations of joint production and the effects of variable service prices on the cost problems of production to a fuller extent than has previously been done. The parallel treatment of the theories of "joint" and "poly-periodic" production is, perhaps, my most original contribution.

In its first form the essay was written at the University of Chicago during the years 1935 and 1936, where at the end of the latter year it was submitted as a dissertation for the doctorate. Since that date it has been revised with regard to style and expression, some parts have been shortened or left out and other parts extended, but in its main contents it remains unchanged.

Because I have been working on problems which have for many years been discussed by economists, I have had a vast literature at my disposal. My indebtedness to this literature for ideas and stimulus is much greater than scattered and specific references can possibly indicate. In a selected bibliography I have tried to indicate the books and articles which have influenced me most. I should mention particularly the works of Frisch, Myrdal, Schneider and Wicksell.

For kindly criticism and valuable comments during the actual process of writing I am greatly indebted to Dr. Tord Palander at the University of Stockholm and to my former professors and fellow students at the University of Chicago: especially the late Professor Henry Schultz, Professors F. H. Knight, J. Viner and T. Yntema, who served as supervisers of my work for the doctorate; and to Messrs. B. Caplan and A. Hart. My sincere thanks are also due to Mrs. Helen Lee Smith, who courageously tried to teach me a most difficult thing, English grammar; to the University College of Commerce, Stockholm, and to the Rockefeller Foundation, New York, whose generous aid in the form of fellowships has made this study possible.

I have been enabled to publish the essay by a grant from the Royal Academy of Science, Stockholm.

University College of Commerce

Stockholm.   June, 1939.

Sune Carlson.

————

CONTENTS.

CHAPTER I.

THE BUSINESS FIRM AND THE PRODUCTION PROCESS.

It is the purpose of the present essay to give a summary of the pure theory of production in its application to the productive activity of the single firm. We shall examine the forces which determine the firm's production and investigate the relationships between costs and revenues and outputs to which these forces give rise. But, before we start our study, we shall state the main assumptions on which the analysis will rest, and classify the problems which we are going to consider.

Some Fundamental Definitions.

1. *Production.* — Among the varied phenomena which are included under the heading of economic activity, we may distinguish two different types of activity and classify them separately: production and exchange. To production we may attribute all the processes of combining and coordinating materials and forces in the creation of some valuable good or service. The goods and services which we classify as the *output* of the production processes are thus thought of as aggregates or sums of physical materials and forces. These materials and forces we shall call the *productive services* or the *input* of the processes. The terms input and output, however, can only be referred to in connection with a particular productive activity, since a good or a service which is an input or productive service in one case, may be an output in another.

The inputs and outputs of a productive process we

shall conceive as *time flows* of determinable physical quantities. They may be hours of labour or of machine service, or tons of steel or copper per year. The production process represents the transformation of input flows into output flows. Besides flows of inputs and outputs, it will sometimes be convenient to speak of *stocks* of goods which are the sources of input flows or are the results of output flows. In its analytical interpretation this concept of a stock is obtained as the sum (integral) of output or input flows during a certain time period. When speaking of inputs the term *productive service* will always be used to signify the time flow concept, and the term *productive resource* to signify the stock concept.

This conception of production as a physical co-ordination of productive services and as a determinable physical time flow of inputs and outputs may in some cases be difficult to apply to actual production phenomena. Some services, like advertising and management, or the services of a patent right, are hard to conceive in quantitative terms either as inputs or as outputs. We may, nevertheless, assume that the individual producer must have at least some idea of their quantitative magnitude.

2. *Business firm.* — The individuals in charge of production we shall call *entrepreneurs;* and a single productive enterprise which is managed by an entrepreneur, such as a bakery or a steel plant, a *technical unit*. The technical unit may also represent an economic unit: the unit over which the entrepreneur has financial control and for which he calculates his total income and investment. Often several technical units are combined in one economic unit, as when the entrepreneur has financial control over several technical units. An economic unit which serves as a unit of financial control we shall refer to as a *business firm*. By definition, the technical unit can never extend beyond the business firm.

3. *Exchange.* — Under the second type of economic activity, the exchange process, we shall include all changes in the conditions of personal ownership that take place in connection with productive activity. With the exception

of capital borrowing and lending, which may be regarded as particular kinds of exchange, the word exchange refers to determinable flows or stocks of goods or services. As has already been pointed out with reference to productive inputs or outputs, a quantitative estimate of such time flows may often cause difficulties, but it may safely be assumed that some estimation takes place in the minds of the trading individuals. Usually goods and services are not exchanged against one another but against one particular good, money, which also serves as a valution standard. The quantitative exchange relation between a time flow, or stock of goods or services measured in physical terms, and money is the *price* of the good or service. Objects which in a competitive market and under identical conditions (with regard to place, time, conditions of sale and payment etc.)[1] have the same price, represent the same good or service.

The exchange value or *money value* of a stock or time flow of a good or service is the product of the physical quantity of the stock or flow and its price. With reference to a production activity, the money value of the input during a certain time period may be considered as the *cost of production* of the activity and the money value of the output as the *production revenue*. Both production costs and production revenues are thus expressed as a sum of money per *period* of time.

4. *Capital funds.* — In order to carry on the production activity the business firm needs capital funds. With reference to their origin these funds may be divided into two separate classes: the capital funds which the firm obtains by borrowing from outsiders — the *borrowed funds* — and the funds which are owned by the firm itself — its

---

[1] A few comments may be needed as regards this definition. We may notice that a good can never be defined by its technical characteristics alone, since these characteristics are always found to vary between any two individual objects if only the inspection is close enough. For the purpose of a price or production analysis (for a utility analysis the case may be different) two classes of objects may be said to constitute the same good if units of them are indifferent to the producers and the consumers; that is, if they are covered by the same supply and demand functions. For an extensive discussion of these problems the reader is referred to J. Drewnowiski. "The classification of Commodities and the Problem of Competition and Monopoly", *Studja Ekonomiczne II* (Cracow, 1935), pp. 41—55.

own funds. The firm may use its capital in three different ways: it may invest it (1) in productive resources (inclusive of "good will"), "goods in process" or finished products in the firm's own productive activity, which may be referred to under a collective name as the firm's *investment in own production,* or (2) in claims on other business firms, for example in the form of bonds or stocks, which may be called *outside investments,* or (3) it may place the funds in *liquid assets,* such as cash money or bank deposits. In many cases, however, it may be difficult to draw a line between these different investment categories: investments in subsidiary companies or trade credits may be both investments in the firm's own production and outside investments, certain bank deposits both outside investments and liquid assets etc.

MONO- AND POLY-PERIODIC PRODUCTION.

1. *Mono-periodic production.* — Throughout the first five chapters of our essay we shall assume that a business firm's production activity is so arranged that the production, the input and output, of one time period is entirely separated from the production of the preceding and subsequent periods. We shall assume that the firm is interested in the activity of only one period at a time, and that this activity is determined exclusively by the conditions prevailing in that period and is independent of any other conditions. The production of such a closed or "self-contained" period we shall refer to as *mono-periodic production.*

In our study of the mono-periodic production we shall make the following assumptions: (a) The production activity starts at a given date and ends at another given date when the output of the production is sold on the market; the time interval between these two dates represents the period under consideration. (b) The business firm buys all productive services necessary for the production of the period on the first day of the period and also pays for the services on that date. The firm's capital funds will consequently be invested in its production during the whole time period; that is, they will first be returned in liquid form on the last day of the period. (c) The remuneration for the use of capital funds, i. e. interest payments on the firm's borrowed funds and dividends on the firm's own capital, is to be paid at the end of the period. This assumption would probably correspond to actual business practice, if we could find examples of the simple type of mono-periodic production here postulated. (d) With regard to the output of the mono-periodic production we shall at first assume that the firm produces one single commodity.[1] Having examined the production problems under these simplifying assumptions, we shall proceed to the case of *joint production;* that is, to the case when several commodities are simultaneously produced.

2. *Poly-periodic production.* — In actual production, however, the different time periods are seldom closed or "self-contained" but are inter-related with one another. Through the existence of durable productive resources, through stocks of "goods in process" and through the interdependence of the price system as between different dates, the production activity in one period is related to the activities of preceding and subsequent periods. A production which in this way is governed not by the conditions of one closed period but by the conditions prevailing in a series of periods is often referred to as capitalistic production, but in order that the particular time relations shall be more strongly emphazied, it will here be called a *poly-periodic production.*

THE PRODUCTION DETERMINING FORCES AND THE PRODUCTION PROBLEMS.

The forces which influence the entrepreneur in his decisions on what to produce and what methods of produc-

---

[1] Since the time period is assumed to be constant, our mono-periodic production differs but slightly from the type of "time-less" production generally discussed in economic literature. But even if the time element in itself is of little importance for the phenomena considered, it is practical to relate the different concepts and relationships to a definite time period from the outset.

tion to use may be classified, with reference to their origin, in four different groups: (1) the demand conditions for finished goods and services existing on the market; (2) the technical knowledge of different combinations possible in producing these goods and services from available productive services; (3) the supply conditions of productive services, and (4) the supply conditions of capital funds. A few comments on the nature of these different forces may be sufficient at this point.

1. *The demand for finished goods and services.* — The demand conditions for finished goods and services inform the entrepreneur about the products that can be sold on the market. To the individual business firm the demand for its output appears as a series of possible price-quantity combinations, whose extent and character depend on the firm's market position. If there are many producers of the same product, the price may appear unique from the single firm's point of view, and the demand for the product at this price will seem infinitely great. If the firm is in a more favourable market position, not only is there a whole series of possible price-quantity combinations but this series may be influenced by the firm through advertising and other kinds of sales promotion. The demand conditions in such a case must therefore be defined in relation to a definite market and definite sales methods. Since the production process requires time and the firm's production has to be planned in advance, it is actually not the demand itself, as it appears on the market, but the entrepreneur's anticipation of this demand at the date of planning, that represents the production determining force.[1]

2. *Technical knowledge.* — If the demand conditions indicate to the entrepreneur what goods may be expected

---

[1] We are concerned here only with the forces and relationships which influence the entrepreneur in the planning of the firm's production; i. e. with the forces and relationships which the entrepreneur *expects to prevail in the future*, not with the forces and relationships actually existing at a given time. Our production analysis is an *ex ante* and not an *ex post* analysis. See G. Myrdal, "Der Gleichgewichtsbegriff als Instrument der geldtheoretischen Analyse", in F. Hayek (ed.), *Beiträge zur Geldtheorie* (Vienna, 1933) p. 394.

to sell on the market, technical knowledge informs him how these goods may be produced. If production is defined as a quantitative process of combining certain given productive services, it is the knowledge of these different possible combinations that we call technical knowledge. Since the entrepreneur has to plan the firm's production in advance, it is the entrepreneur's knowledge of the technical conditions as they exist at the date of planning that is important. Unforeseen changes in the technical processes taking place after the planning date are without effect on the firm's production.

3. *The supply of productive services.* — The supply of productive services, like the demand for finished products, appears to the individual firm as a series of price-quantity combinations. In the case where the firm's demand for a productive service is negligible in comparison with the total demand for the factor, the price is constant and an infinitely great quantity can be obtained at that price. On the other hand, when the firm's demand represents a considerable part of the total demand for a service, a larger quantity of the service can often be obtained only at an increasing price. As in the case of demand conditions for the firm's output, it is not the service supply actually prevailing at any particular date, but the entrepreneur's anticipation of this service supply that represents the production determining factor.

4. *The supply of capital funds.* — The supply of capital funds for a particular production activity is determined by two sets of circumstances, those regulating the total supply of capital to the business firm, and those regulating the investment of funds in other activities. The firm's total capital, we should remember, is equal to the sum of its own capital funds and its borrowed funds. We shall assume that at any given date the firm's own funds are fixed in amount, and that the total capital can be increased only by an increase in its borrowed funds. The price of such an increase is the rate of interest. With given anticipations with regard to the capital supply, the capital applied to a particular productive activity will be deter-

mined by the rate of return the firm expects from the activity and the expected rate of return from outside investments.

5. *The production problems of the business firm.* — Our task in the following chapters is to examine how the different production determining forces here outlined influence the management of the firm's productive activity. The goal of this activity, it may be assumed, is to obtain a maximum net return on the firm's capital. By considering the production determining forces, first separately, and then together, we shall proceed with our study in three different steps, and distinguish between three separate types of production problems: (1) The *technical problems* of production which correspond to the technical knowledge, are concerned with the quantitative relations between input of productive services and output of products, measured in physical units. (2) The *cost problems* of production, which assume the technical relationships between input and output as given, deal with the relations between the costs of different inputs and the quantity of output measured in physical terms. The cost problems are related to three classes of production determining forces: the technical knowledge, the supply of productive services, and the supply of capital funds. (3) Finally, the *maximization problems* of production, by which we mean the maximization of the net return, pertain to the cost problems in their relation to the problems of demand and revenue. These problems are concerned with how all four of the production determining forces in combination determine the firm's production.

With this review of our definitions and assumptions and classification of the production determining forces and the problems of production, we may proceed to our main analysis. In the next three chapters we shall be concerned with what we have defined as simple monoperiodic production. Chapter II will be devoted to technical problems, chapter III to cost problems, and chapter IV to maximization problems under this form of production.

In chapter V we shall examine the case of joint production, but still under mono-periodic assumptions. We shall not take up the more difficult problems of poly-periodic production until chapter VI, the final chapter of our essay.

CHAPTER II.

INPUT AND OUTPUT.

The technical problems of production are concerned with the quantitative relationship between input of productive services and output of products measured in physical terms. They deal with the production determining forces which we have classified under the heading of "technical knowledge". Viewed by themselves, the technical problems of production are problems in engineering rather than in economics. They present data for, but are not themselves a part of the purely economic analysis of production. The purpose of the present chapter is, therefore, not so much to examine the technical relationships between input and output in all their details — that we leave for the engineers — as to present these relationships in a form useful for a later economic analysis. The chapter contains but little that is not common knowledge to the student of modern production theory.

THE TECHNICAL UNIT.

1. *The technical unit.* — The unit for which the entrepreneur calculates his profit and investments; that is, the unit of financial control, we have called the business firm. This unit is not necessarily the same as the unit for which the entrepreneur calculates the costs of production. The cost calculations of a business firm may generally be simplified by considering separately the different parts of the firm: that is, by making separate cost calculations for the plants or departments, here termed technical units. If we consider the case of a sawmill's production, for example, it may be convenient to consider the sawing process as one techni-

cal unit, the planing as another, the power production as still a third, and to calculate the production costs accordingly. The technical relationship between service input and product output may then be determined for each of these units separately.[1] Our present study will be concerned with the inputs and outputs of *one* such technical unit.

2. *Output and input.* — In this and the two following chapters we shall be concerned with a mono-periodic production: we shall assume that the production of the technical unit takes place inside a closed time period, and is determined exclusively by the conditions prevailing in that period. We shall further assume that the *output* of the technical unit, which by assumption is sold at the end of the period, consists of a single commodity; that is, we shall assume a case of simple mono-periodic production.

---

[1] If we symbolize the different technical units by rectangles, and the inputs and outputs by arrows to and from the rectangles, the sawmill's production may be pictured:

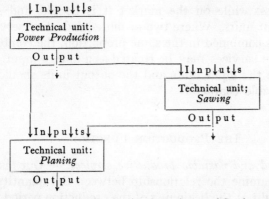

The output of Power Production is an input of Sawing and Planing; the output of Sawing is another input of Planing.

If we disregard the problem of allocation of certain joint costs to the different technical units, the cost calculations and the profit maximization become considerably simpler when the firm's production is divided into such units, than if the calculations were carried through with the business firm as a single unit; that is, if only the ("external") relationships between the services actually bought and the product actually sold on the market were considered. Such a division of the firm's production in calculation units is generally made in the practical cost accounting. Compare, for example, the accounting system of the packing industry as described by G. E. Putnam. "Joint Cost in the Packing Industry", *Journal of Political Economy* XXIX (1921) pp. 293—303.

As regards the productive services which constitute the *input* to the technical unit during the period we shall only consider the services which are limited in supply. When a productive service is abundant and costs nothing, it does not enter into the business firm's calculations, even though it may be essential to the firm's production. In practice it would be most difficult for a firm to enumerate the necessary services which are freely obtainable. It is only when a productive service becomes sufficiently limited to be priced, that its importance is noticed.

The definition of a unit for measurement of service input and product output must be made with regard to the practicability of calculation in each particular case. The service and product units used by the business firm in its cost and profit calculations need in no way be identical with the market units of the services or products. The input of fuel in a certain productive process may, for instance, be figured in calories in its relationship to the output of the process; while on the market it is bought and sold by different units. Where two or more productive services are always combined in the same proportion, the combination of the services may be treated as a unit of input. In every case the input units and the output units should be of measurable character.

THE PRODUCTION FUNCTION.

1. *Fixed and variable productive services.* — Our task is now to examine the relationship between the quantity of input bought at the beginning of the production period and the quantity of output turned out by the process at the period's end. Among the productive services that constitute the input, we shall distinguish two different kinds: the services that vary and the services that do not vary with the amount of product produced. The former we shall refer to as the *variable productive services*, the latter as the *fixed services* or merely as the *plant*. Examples of variable productive services are raw materials and "direct labor";

examples of fixed services are certain machine services or the services of a factory building.

The variability or constancy of a productive service may be technical in nature: the input of coal or iron to a process, for instance, may be technically variable, while the input of a certain machine service is technically fixed. It is, however, not the technical variability in itself, but the fixed or variable cost of the service that is important in this connection. Some productive services may be technically variable and still represent fixed costs. For example: a firm contracts to buy a certain amount of electric current: the input of this current is regulated at the will of the entrepreneur, but the cost of the current is fixed by the contract. Other services may be technically fixed, but represent variable costs. This type of service is illustrated by shoe machines or statistical tabulation machines that are paid for not by the month or year but by the amount of work done. It is the *effect on the firm's costs* and not the technical characteristics that determine whether a productive service should be classified as variable or fixed.

In practice a sharp dividing line seldom exists between the variable and fixed productive services. The fixed services are generally fixed when the output varies only within certain limits. When the output increases beyond that limit, some services, for example the services of a factory building, may still be fixed; but others, for example machine services, must be increased.[1] Still it is convenient to distinguish between the two groups, and to examine the effect of the variable productive services on output

---

[1] Speaking about production costs J. M. Clark [*The Economics of Overhead Costs*, (Chicago, 1923) p. 229] observes: "Instead of merely saying that a certain part of the expenses are »constant,» care should always be taken to say that a certain part of the expenses are unaffected by such-and-such a change in volume of business." B. Ohlin distinguishes between *three* classes of costs: (1) fixed costs which remain constant inside very wide ranges of output; (2) continuously variable costs which vary with all changes in output, and (3) intermittently variable costs which vary discontinuously as soon as the output passes certain limits. (See "Omkostnadsanalys och Prispolitik", Mimeographed lectures, Stockholm, 1934, pp. 13—18.) In order to make our analysis the simplest possible we have brought together both the services that correspond to Ohlin's "fixed costs" and the services that correspond to his "intermittently variable costs" under the heading of fixed services or plant.

separately from the effect caused by changes in the plant.

Throughout the mono-periodic analysis we have assumed that all productive services, that is, both the variable services and the plant, are bought at the beginning of the time period, and that none of them lasts for more than one period's activity. The distinction between durable and non-durable productive resources is therefore of no concern here. It may be postponed to the study of poly-periodic production.

2. *The production function.* — When we now proceed to our study of the technical production problem we shall examine the relationship between the variable productive services and the output under the assumption that the plant remains constant; that is, that there exists a given equipment of factory building, machine services, "contracted" services, etc. This relationship we may most conveniently express in mathematical form, writing the amount of output as a function of the different variable services. If we denote the quantity of output by x, and the quantities of the variable productive services, n in number, by $v_1 \ldots v_n$, we write:

$$(1) \qquad x = \varphi(v_1, \ldots, v_n).$$

This in our *production function*. The production function, it must be remembered, is defined in relation to a given plant; that is certain fixed services.

A given amount of output may frequently be produced from a number of different service combinations. It may also be true that the same combination of productive services gives varied amounts of output, depending upon how efficiently the productive services are organized. The output of an automobile factory, for instance, may vary for different organizations of the same workers and tools on the assembly line. If we want the production function to give only one value for the output from a given service combination, the function must be so defined that it expresses the *maximum product* obtainable from the combination at the existing state of technical knowledge.[1] Therefore, the purely *technical* maximization problem may be said to be solved by the very definition of our production function.[2]

This definition of the production function implies that the technical organization of the productive services may vary when the service combinations and output vary. The optimum organization is seldom the same for different amounts of output. If, in an automobile factory, the output is to be a hundred cars a week, the optimum organisation of tools and workers is quite different from what it would be for a thousand cars. A change in the technical organization of the productive services which accompanies a change in the output must not, of course, be confused with a change in the technical knowledge. A change in the former is a reversible process; a change in the latter is not. When, after a change, a group of productive services revert to their initial combination, the optimal technical organization and the optimal output from the combination will be the same as before the first change took place, provided the technical knowledge is constant.

---

[1] Cf. F. Y. Edgeworth, "The Laws of Increasing and Diminishing Returns," *Papers Relating to Political Economy* (London, 1925), I, p. 69: "In this presumption it is taken for granted that the entrepreneur applies his outlay to the best of his ability in order to obtain the greatest possible profit."

[2] To this technical maximization problem belongs, under our present assumptions, the question of how the different productive services should be timed in relation to one another. The "time-table of production", we assume is determined only by technical considerations. But this holds true only for mono-periodic production, where all the productive services are assumed to be bought at the same time. In poly-periodic production, where the productive services are bought at different dates, we shall find that the interest rate and the relative service prices of the different dates enter as determining factors.

We shall notice, however, that even under our mono-periodic assumptions there exists at least one "time problem" of production that is economic in nature: namely, whether to increase the input under conditions of an unchanged working day, or to increase the number of working hours per day. Into this problem we shall not enter here, but assume that the number of hours per working day is fixed. For a discussion of this question the reader is referred to A. Smithies, "The Austrian Theory of Capital in Relation to Partial Equilibrium Theory", *Quarterly Journal of Economics*, (1935/36) pp. 126 ff. and E. Schneider, "Arbeitszeit und Produktion", *Archiv für math. Wirtschafts- und Sozialforschung*, I (1935) pp. 23 ff. and p. 137 ff.

For every service combination there exists one and only one optimal organization and only one maximum output. A change in technical knowledge, on the other hand, implies that the optimal organization and the maximum output from *the same* service combination have changed.[1]

Before we proceed with our analysis of the production function we shall introduce two analytical concepts which will greatly facilitate our study. The first of these concepts is the marginal productivity and the second the function coefficient.

3. *Marginal productivity*. — The partial derivative of the production function with respect to a productive service v_k

$$\frac{\partial x}{\partial v_k} = \varphi_{v_k}$$

we shall refer to as the *marginal productivity of v_k* and the differential product $dx_{(v_k)}$ which is obtained from an infinitesimal increment of v_k while the other productive services remain constant

$$dx_{(v_k)} = \varphi_{v_k} dv_k$$

we shall call the *marginal product* of the increment dv_k. If this increment is equal to unity the marginal product and the marginal productivity of the service are evidently the same.

It is clear that any infinitesimal variation of the productive services may be thought of as an aggregate of individual service variations. Consequently the change in output produced by any arbitrary but infinitesimal service variation, can be written as the sum of the marginal products of the individual services

$$(2) \qquad dx = \varphi_{v_1} dv_1 + \ldots + \varphi_{v_n} dv_n.[2]$$

---

[1] A definition of "constant technical knowledge" is exceedingly difficult to give in any actual production process since the maximal technical organizations for the whole range of possible service combinations are seldom known in advance but have to be found out by practical experience.

[2] For a more rigorous mathematical proof of this relationship the reader is referred to the textbooks on calculus. See e. g. F. S. Woods, *Advanced Calculus* (Boston, 1934), p. 78.

4. *The function coefficient and proportional return.* — As the quantity of output does or does not vary in proportion to a proportional change in all the productive services the production in question will be said to yield a constant or variable *proportional return.* As a scale of measure of the proportional return we shall introduce the concept of *function coefficient.*[1] If the productive services obtain a proportional increment $dv_1 = mv_1$, $dv_2 = mv_2 \ldots$ etc. which causes the output to vary by an amount dx, the function coefficient ε expresses the relationship between the relative variations of output and productive services

$$\varepsilon = \frac{dx}{x} : \frac{dv_k}{v_k} = \frac{dx}{x} : m$$

$$k = 1, \ldots, n$$

The change in output dx caused by the proportional increment of the services is expressed by

$$dx = \varphi_{v_1} mv_1 + \ldots + \varphi_{v_n} mv_n$$

and when $\varepsilon x m$ is substituted for dx this gives us the important relationship

(3) $$x \varepsilon = \varphi_{v_1} v_1 + \ldots + \varphi_{v_n} v_n.$$

That is, when the service variations are proportional the quantity of output multiplied by the function coefficient is always equal to the sum of the quantities of the productive services multiplied by their respective marginal productivities. In the case of constant proportional return the change in output caused by a proportional service variation is by definition

$$dx = mx$$

from which it follows that the function coefficient is unity and that equation (3) may be written

---

[1] The same concept is referred to by Johnson as the "elasticity of production", by Frisch as "passus koefficient" and by Schneider as "Ergiebigkeitsgrad". Cf. W. E. Johnson, "The Pure Theory of Utility Curves", *Economic Journal*, XXIII (1913). p. 507, R. Frisch, "Tekniske og økonomiske Produktivitetslover", mimeographed lectures, University of Oslo, § 637, and E. Schneider, *Theorie der Produktion*, Wien, 1934. p. 10.

18

(3a)
$$x = \varphi_{v_1} v_1 + \ldots + \varphi_{v_n} v_n{}^1$$

After the introduction of these concepts and relationships
we shall proceed with our study of the production function.

GRAPHIC REPRESENTATION OF PRODUCTION.

1. *The production diagram.* — If we assume a production with only two variable services, the production
function

$$x = \varphi (v_1, v_2)$$

may be represented by a surface in a three dimensional
diagram. An example of such a production surface is given

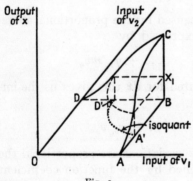

Fig. 1.

in fig. 1. The inputs of
the services are plotted on
the base axes v_1 and v_2
and the vertical axis x
gives the maximum out-
put corresponding to the
combinations of services
on the base plane. Thus
the surface $OACD$ repre-
sents the locus of the outputs of all possible service
combinations. When one
of the services is kept con-

stant, e. g. v_1 at the quantity OA, the output is shown
to increase with the amount of the other service along
the curve AC. The rate of change of this curve, that
is, the partial rate of change of the output with respect
to service v_2, is the graphic representation of the marginal productivity of v_2 for a value of v_1 equal to OA

---

[1] For a further discussion of this relationship and its implication in
the theory of distribution the reader is referred to the works of Wicksteed,
Wicksell, Johnson, Hicks and others. Compare in particular P. H.
Wicksteed, *The Co-ordination of the Laws of Distribution*, (London, 1894)
Knut Wicksell, *Lectures on Political Economy* (Engl. transl. New York,
1934) Vol. I pp. 124 ff. and "Den 'kritiska punkten' i lagen för jordbruket
aftagande produktivitet", *Ekonomisk Tidskrift* XVIII (1916) pp. 285—92
W. E. Johnson, "The Pure Theory of Utility Curves", *op. cit.* pp. 506 ff

19

Correspondingly the slope of the curve *DC* represents the marginal productivity of v_1 when v_2 is equal to *OD*.

Such a graphic illustration of the production function is possible of course only in the case of two variable services. However, since most of the relationships governing the production process are the same irrespective of the number of productive services, or, since in the case of several services one may proceed to study the production relations taking only two services at a time, the graphic analysis will have a much wider applicability to the technical problems of production than might at first be thought.

2. *The isoquants.* — Although there exists only one maximum output for every combination of variable services, a given output may be obtained from a series of different service combinations. In fig. 1, for example, the output x_1 is produced by all combinations along the curve $A'D'$. Such a curve combining all services which yield the same output is generally called a production indifference curve or an *isoquant.* For every output we may draw one isoquant, and one isoquant — but only one — may be passed through every service combination on the $v_1 - v_2$ plane. Consequently no isoquants can intersect one another; they constitute concentric curves at different distances from the point of origin. Further, since a larger output requires a larger input of variable services than a smaller output, an isoquant which represents a larger output must always lie farther away from the point of origin than an isoquant representing a smaller output. Thus in fig. 2 the output x_3 is larger than the output x_2 and this output in its turn is larger than x_1. Through the establishment of such a system of isoquants we may dispense with the more cumbersome three dimen-

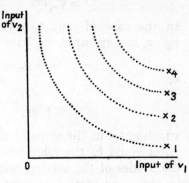

Fig. 2.

sional production diagram in fig. 1 and illustrate the variation in output caused by different changes in the inputs of
the services by movements relative to the different isoquants. Thus an increase in output is represented by a
movement from a lower to a higher isoquant, a constant
output by a change along a given isoquant and a decrease
by a shift from a higher isoquant to a lower.

The equation of the isoquant system is obtained directly
from the production function

$$x_o = \varphi(v_1, \ldots, v_n)$$

where x_o represents the constant output of each particular
isoquant, or from the differential of this function

$$0 = \varphi_{v_1} dv_1 + \ldots + \varphi_{v_n} dv_n.$$

In the case of only two variable services illustrated in
fig. 2, for example, we have

$$0 = \varphi_{v_1} dv_1 + \varphi_{v_2} dv_2$$

or

$$\frac{dv_2}{dv_1} = -\frac{\varphi_{v_1}}{\varphi_{v_2}}$$

which gives us the slope of the isoquant at any particular
point equal to the relationship between the marginal productivities of the services with a minus sign. The change
in the slope of the isoquants as one service is increased
while the other service remains constant is given by the
second derivatives

$$\frac{\partial}{\partial v_1}\left(\frac{dv_2}{dv_1}\right) = -\frac{\varphi_{v_2}\varphi_{v_1 v_1} - \varphi_{v_1}\varphi_{v_1 v_2}}{\varphi_{v_2}^2}$$

and

$$\frac{\partial}{\partial v_2}\left(\frac{dv_2}{dv_1}\right) = -\frac{\varphi_{v_2}\varphi_{v_1 v_2} - \varphi_{v_1}\varphi_{v_2 v_2}}{\varphi_{v_2}^2}$$

and the change in the slope along a given isoquant by the
derivative

$$\frac{d^2v_2}{dv_1^2} = \frac{\partial}{\partial v_1}\left(\frac{dv_2}{dv_1}\right) + \frac{\partial}{\partial v_2}\left(\frac{dv_2}{dv_1}\right) \cdot \frac{dv_2}{dv_1}$$

$$= -\frac{\varphi_{v_1 v_1}\varphi_{v_2}^2 + 2\varphi_{v_1 v_2}\varphi_{v_1}\varphi_{v_2} - \varphi_{v_2 v_2}\varphi_{v_1}^2}{\varphi_{v_2}^3}$$

Thus there is an intimate relationship between the properties of the isoquant pattern and the properties of the marginal productivities. Before we proceed with our study of these relationships it will, however, be desirable to reconsider the question of the proportional service variations and their influence on the output.

3. *The proportional service variations and the properties of the function coefficient.* — A production has been said to yield a constant or variable proportional return according as the quantity of output does or does not vary in proportion to a proportional service variation. At first one may think that constant proportional return should be prevalent in all productions, since it seems rather natural that the output should be doubled, trebled, and so on when the input of all the services is increased twice, three times etc. But there are two phenomena generally occurring in actual production which prevent this from happening. The first one which we have already observed is that a proportional service variation can very seldom be extended to include all the productive services. There exist in almost every line of production some services — the plant or the fixed services — which the business firm cannot vary at will or at least not vary continuously. The second phenomenon which gives rise to variable proportional return is the fact, also noticed above, that the maximal technical organization of the productive services usually varies with a variation of the input. An increased input of the productive services commonly permits a more efficient organization, at least on the purely technical side of production; a more extensive division and specialization of labour, for instance, may be possible. On the side of business management, however, the tendency may be reversed, particularly with larger service inputs. The leadership and control of the business firm and its commercial relations frequently become increasingly difficult when the size of the firm has passed a certain limit.[1]

---

[1] The existence of variable proportional returns may thus be attributed to the fact that it is not always possible to divide the productive services in the most efficient way. If the services were fully divisible, not only would the fixed services be non-existent, but the technical organization

If we consider the combined influence of these circumstances on the relationship between the proportional service variations and the output in a hypothetical production, we may illustrate this relationship graphically as in fig. 3. Starting out from a particular combination of the variable services (v_1', v_2' fig. 3B), we let these services increase proportionally while the fixed services remain constant:

$$v_1 = mv_1'$$
$$v_2 = mv_2'$$

where m increases gradually. During the first part of this service increase, the output is assumed to increase more

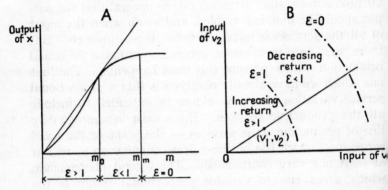

Fig. 3.

than proportionally to the services (see fig. 3A); that is, the function coefficient is assumed to be greater than unity and the proportional return to be increasing. Better exploitation of the fixed services and better organization of the productive services will have an accelerating effect on the output. After a particular input (m_0v_1', m_0v_2') is reached, however, the relative limitation of the fixed services and the increasing difficulties of the business

would also be just as efficient for small inputs as for large. Compare Joan Robinson, *The Economics of Imperfect Competition* (London, 1934), p. 335, n. 1: "The increase in efficiency which arises from the fact that 'practice makes perfect' is itself a result of the indivisibility of the units of the factors. If labour could be finally divided, like sand, each grain of labour could be occupied constantly at a single task and could acquire the maximum amount of practice."

management will begin to retard the increase of the output. The function coefficient will fall below unity and the proportional return will decrease. At a certain later input $(m_m v_1', m_m v_2')$ finally, the output will cease to increase and the function coefficient and the proportional return will be zero. An increase of the variable services beyond this limit will not increase the output as long as the fixed services remain constant, nor will it decrease the output since the services will always be organized in such a way that the maximum output is obtained.

Just as we have related the output to a proportional service variation through the combination (v_1', v_2'), we may relate the output to a proportional service variation through any given service combination with a similar result. Thus, on every straight line passing from the point of origin we shall have points at which the function coefficient changes from greater than unity to less than unity, and from positive values to zero. By combining these points by curves we may divide the diagram into areas of increasing, decreasing and zero proportional return (see fig. 3B). We must keep in mind, however, that the nature of the proportional return and the properties of the function coefficient are technical data to be determined in the particular case from practical experience, and that the pattern which we have here described is to be regarded as an example only.

4. *Three types of isoquant patterns.* — After this excursion into the proportional service variations and their influence on output let us return to our study of the isoquants. Here also we shall be dealing with relationships which in actual production are a part of the technical data. Our task therefore is not to enumerate and describe all the different types of isoquant patterns which may actually be found, but merely to illustrate a few very simple relations which are of particular theoretical interest.[1]

---

[1] An interesting attempt to construct isoquants empirically by use of statistical data from chocolate production has been made by Ragnar Frisch ["The Principle of Substitution. An Example of its Application in the Chocolate Industry," *Nordisk Tidskrift for Teknisk Økonomi*, I (1935), pp. 12—27].

24

We shall first consider a production in which by technical necessity the variable services are always combined in certain proportions. When the output is given, the minimum input of every individual service required is also given and it is impossible to substitute one service for another.[1] As an example let us take the production of a chemical compound where two raw materials (the variable services v_1 and v_2, fig. 4) enter into the process in constant

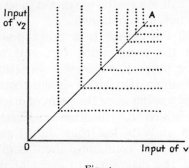

Fig. 4.

proportions (illustrated by the straight line OA).[2] Since an increase in output by assumption requires a proportional increase of both of the variable services, an addition in the input of only one of the services to a combination on OA will have no effect on the output, that is, the marginal productivity of the service in question will be zero.[3] The isoquants passing through different points of OA must consequently consist of straight lines parallel to the axes and at right angles to one another. But it is of course only the service combinations on OA which will be of any interest to the entrepreneur, since these combinations represent the minimum inputs for every possible output. On OA the relationship between input and output is determined by the properties of the function coefficient discussed in the preceding section.

[1] This is the case well known from Walras and Cassel of fixed "coefficients of production".

[2] In theory this example may be regarded as a variety of a more general case in which the variable services are combined in given but not necessarily constant proportions (i. e. when OA is any type of curve). It would probably be difficult, however, to find examples of productions where the service combinations for different outputs are technically given but the proportions between the services varying.

[3] Since the quantity of output is thus limited by the amount of the variable service kept constant, Frisch refers to this service as a *limitatio service* ("Einige Punkte einer Preistheorie mit Boden und Arbeit a' Produktionsfaktoren," *Zeitschrift für Nationalökonomie*, III (1932), 1 64 and "Tekniske og økonomiske Produktivitetslover" *op. cit.*).

As a second case let us examine a production where the technical relations between inputs and output are of the reverse character to those just considered; a production in which the variable services are perfectly substitutable for one another. A given output is then obtained not from a technically given minimum combination of the services but from a whole series of combinations so constituted that a unit change in one of the services requires a constant and opposite change in another service. Take as example a production in which adult labour is perfectly substitutable for juvenile labour. Since the substitutability is perfect the relationship between the marginal productivities of the services must be the same. The isoquants conse-

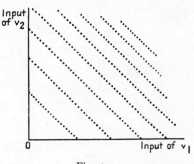

Fig. 5.

quently have a constant slope and are straight lines parallel to one another, as is indicated in fig. 5. The marginal productivity of one of the services as related to an increase in that individual service will be determined by the properties of the function coefficient; it will be increasing, constant or decreasing according as the function coefficient is greater than, equal to, or smaller than unity. But when the marginal productivity of one of the services changes, the marginal productivity of the other service will change in an equal porportion, leaving the relation between the two always the same.[1]

In an actual production we shall probably find most of the variable services to be neither technically given nor perfectly substitutable. The relationship between the ser-

---

[1] Using the same notation as before, we have

$$\frac{\varphi_{v_1 v_1}}{\varphi_{v_1}} = \frac{\varphi_{v_1 v_2}}{\varphi_{v_2}} \text{ and } \frac{\varphi_{v_2 v_2}}{\varphi_{v_2}} = \frac{\varphi_{v_2 v_1}}{\varphi_{v_1}}$$

from which it follows that all the second derivatives on page 20 will be zero.

vices and the output is generally much more complicated. In agriculture, for example, it is found that the same amount of wheat may be obtained from different combinations of land, cultivation, fertilizer and grain,[1] or in a metallurgical refining process the same quantity of metal may be extracted at different combinations of smelting temperature and ore quantities, but the substitutability between the services is seldom perfect and does not exist

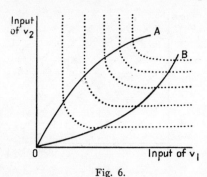

Fig. 6.

for all service combinations. A constant increase in smelting temperature may compensate only inside very narrow limits for a unit diminution of ore, and vice versa. If the output is to remain constant a continuous decrease in ore quantity will probably require an ever increasing rise in temperature until another limit is reached where a further rise will no longer affect the output. In their simplest form these relationships may be illustrated as in fig. 6. Between the limits set by the border lines OA and OB the two services v_1 and v_2 are substitutable but not completely so. A gradual diminution of one of the services requires a continuously increasing addition to the other service. Thus, a movement towards the border line OB will decrease the marginal productivity of v_1 and increase the marginal productivity of v_2, and a movement towards the border line OA will have the opposite effect. Above OA and below OB the marginal productivities of v_2 and v_1 respectively are zero and the isoquants are consequently straight lines parallel to the axes just as in the case of technically fixed service combinations. In the area between the two border lines, on the other hand, where the two services

---

[1] Cf. H. R. Tolley, J. D. Black and M. J. B. Ezekiel, "Input as Related to Output", *U. S. Dept. of Agriculture, Bull. No. 1277* (1924) and J. Warming, *Landbrugets Grænse-Kalkulationer* (Copenhagen, 1933).

are substitutable, the marginal productivities of both services will be positive, and it is only between combinations inside this area that the entrepreneur's choice will stand.

A comparison between the three isoquant patterns here described makes it clear that the first two should be regarded merely as special varieties of the third. The case of technically given combinations in fig. 4 is obtained if the two border lines in fig. 6 gradually approach each other till they finally coincide, and the case of perfectly interchangeable services in fig. 5, if the border lines depart from each other and become identical with the axes at the same time as the isoquants get flatter and flatter. The pattern in fig. 6 is the most general of the three and it is to this pattern that we shall refer when in the following we wish to illustrate our findings with respect to a system of isoquants.

5. *The isoclines.* — If for any particular combination of variable services we indicate the marginal productivities of the services with arrows in the direction of the axes, we may characterize all the marginal productivities by a single resultant of these arrows (see fig. 7). The slope of the resultant expresses the proportion between the marginal productivities. In the isoquant pattern of the type just

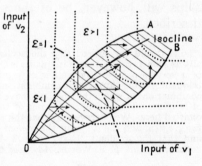

Fig. 7.

discussed this slope of the resultant will be positive for all service combinations inside the two border lines OA and OB, horizontal for all combinations on the line OA, and vertical for all combinations on OB. Frisch refers to this slope as the *productivity direction* of the service combination, and to curves, like OA and OB, which combine all the service combinations with the same productivity direction as *isoclines*.[1] As we shall find in the next chapter,

[1] *Op. cit.* § 633.

the variations of the productive services along the different isoclines are of great importance for the output adjustments of the firm. On their way through the diagram the isoclines will pass areas of increasing and decreasing proportional return, as indicated in the figure, but these returns are defined, we must remember, not with regard to the variations along the isoclines but to the proportional service variations, which do not necessarily have to be the same.[1] In fact, the isocline and the proportional service variations are generally the same only in the case of constant proportional return.

With this discussion of the isoclines we conclude our study of the purely technical relationships of production. We should notice that all these relationships have been defined to a given plant or a given set of fixed productive services. For changed values of the fixed services we should have other production functions and other relationships between input and output. The nature of these relationships will, however, be of the same character as is here described.

---

[1] It should be noticed that the isoclines may be constructed graphically as soon as the system of isoquants is given. The productivity direction of a service combination stands at right angles to the tangent of the isoquant passing through the combination. Thus if we combine the service combinations at which the isoquants have the same slope we get the system of isoclines. The geometrical proof of this relationship is simple and is omitted here. We observe only that the productivity direction represents the *gradient* and the isoquant the *contour line* of the production function, and that the gradient always takes a direction which is normal to the contour line (cf. F. S. Woods, *Advanced Calculus, op. cit.* pp. 74—77).

CHAPTER III.

COSTS OF PRODUCTION.

In the last chapter we were concerned with the purely physical relations between input and output. We shall now examine the price aspects of these relations. As before, we shall consider only the productive services and the prices of these services; we shall disregard the existence of interest costs. Since under our present mono-periodic assumptions the interest costs are always proportional to the costs of the productive services, the interest costs have but little effect on the various relationships considered in the present chapter. We shall therefore postpone the examination of the interest costs till the beginning of the next chapter. Before we begin our cost analysis, we shall say a few words about the supply conditions of the productive services.

The Supply of Productive Services.

We have assumed in our mono-periodic production that the business firm buys the productive services necessary for its production at the time when the productive activity commences. It is the anticipated supply conditions on the market at this date that influence the entrepreneur in his cost calculations. We shall assume that the service prices are quoted per physical unit of the services, and not, as they sometimes are in actual industry, in relation to the amount of output produced (e. g. piece-work).[1]

---

[1] We may notice that if all the productive services were paid in relation to the output produced, the purely technical relationships between input and output would be of no direct relevance to the cost problems of production. It is because some productive services — in our analysis all the services — are paid per unit of service, that the cost analysis has to be based on a knowledge of the technical relationships.

1. *The price functions.* — When the firm buys only a small part of the total quantity of a productive service that is marketed, the price of this service will generally be independent of the amount bought. The price will appear as a constant in the firm's cost calculations. When the firm buys a larger part of the prevailing supply, the price generally varies with the service quantity bought. In this case we may say that the price of the service is a function of the quantity. Thus, if v_k is the amount of the service purchased by the firm, and q_k its price, we may write

$$q_k = q_k (v_k).$$

We shall assume that there exists no "price discrimination" on the buying market; that is, that the firm has no possibility of buying one part of the service quantity at a lower price and another part at a higher price. The price, q_k, is the anticipated average price per unit of the service and the price which the entrepreneur actually expects to pay. We shall start with the assumption that the price function is continuous and single-valued.[1] Often, however, the price does not in practice vary continuously with the amount of the service bought, but in an irregular fashion. Electric current or freight service, for instance, may sometimes be bought in small quantities at one price, and in large quantities at a different price. In addition to our analysis of continuous price changes, we shall therefore have to consider the effects of such irregular price variations.

2. *Price flexibility.* — When a service price is a continuous function of the quantity bought, the rate of change of the price, expressed in absolute terms, is obtained as the derivative of the price function

$$\frac{dq_k}{dv_k} = \frac{dq_k (v_k)}{dv_k}.$$

This derivative may be positive or negative, according as the service price increases or decreases with the amount

---

[1] We shall also assume that the price of one service depends on the quantity of that service only, and is independent of the quantities of the other services; that is, we shall disregard the possible existence of a joint price relation between the different services.

purchased. Examples of services with increasing supply prices may be found in "unskilled labor" or in raw materials. Examples of services with decreasing supply prices are services which are produced under conditions of decreasing costs. In addition to the derivative of the price function which expresses the rate of price change in absolute terms we shall introduce the concept of *price flexibility* as a measure of the *relative* rate of price variation

$$\lambda = \frac{dq_k}{q_k} : \frac{dv_k}{v_k} = \frac{dq_k}{dv_k} \cdot \frac{v_k}{q_k} \cdot {}^1 \quad = \frac{1}{\eta_k}$$

The inverse value of this price flexibility we recognize as the "elasticity of supply", a concept often used in the Anglo-Saxon literature of the subject. When the price increases with the service quantity bought the price flexibility is positive; when the price decreases, the price flexibility is negative. In other words, the price flexibility has the sign of the derivative of the price function. The absolute value of the price flexibility is determined by the properties of the price function. Theoretically it may have any value greater than minus one.[2]

THE EXPANSION PATH.

In the present part of our study we are assuming throughout that the business firm purchases on the market all the

---

[1] See H. L. Moore, *Synthetic Economics* (New York, 1929), p. 38.

[2] When the price is a decreasing function of the service quantity, it is most unlikely that the price flexibility is less than minus unity, i. e. that the service supply is "inelastic". If the price flexibility is less than minus one, the seller of the productive service will receive less revenue from a greater quantity than from a smaller. Using the same symbols as before we may express the rate of change in the revenue as

$$\frac{d(q_k v_k)}{dv_k} = q_k + v_k \frac{dq_k}{dv_k} = q_k(1 + \lambda_k):$$

and this quantity is negative when λ_k is less than minus unity.

If the price is falling because the seller of the service operates his production under conditions of "internal economies", there can be no competition on the selling market, and an individual seller can never, of course, be expected to increase his sale if he will thereby receive a smaller revenue. On the other hand, if the price is falling because of "external economies" of production, it seems unlikely that these economies can be great enough to produce a price flexibility less than minus unity.

different productive services used in its production. The money outlays for these purchases represent the firm's costs of production. The production costs are thus directly related to the inputs of the productive services; and through the technical relationships between input and output, they are related to the quantity of output produced. On the basis of our previous discussion of the technical relationships and of the supply conditions of the productive services we shall now examine these different cost relations.

1. *The marginal unit costs and the cost-productivity ratios.* We observed in the preceding chapter that a certain output can generally be produced from a number of different service combinations — from all the combinations on a given isoquant. Since the prices of these combinations can seldom be expected to be the same, there will usually exist a whole series of possible costs related to every output. The first object of the entrepreneur's cost calculations, therefore, is to find the service combinations which have the lowest costs; not until this is done can he determine his total costs for different levels of output.[1]

If we want to examine the properties of the minimum cost combinations for a certain output, we need only consider the costs of the variable services. The plant or the fixed services, we have assumed, are constant for the range of outputs under consideration, and the costs of these services are also constant. Consequently they do not affect the choice of minimum cost combinations. We may arrive at the minimum cost for a given output through a process of gradual substitution between the different variable services. At the substitution margin a unit increase in the input of a service (v_k) will have a certain cost which we shall call its *marginal unit cost* (c_k). The addition in the quantity of output caused by a unit increase of the individual service we have earlier defined as the marginal

---

[1] In most business firms it is this latter problem that is generally handled by the cost accountants, while the calculations of the minimum cost combinations are left to the production manager. It is probably the division of these tasks and their allotment to different persons which is the reason why the questions of minimum cost combinations have been given so little attention in cost accounting literature.

productivity of the service $\left(\varphi_{v_k}\right)$. The relationship between the marginal unit cost of the productive service and its marginal productivity gives us the rate of change of the costs of production as related to a unit increment of a single service. This relationship we shall define as the *cost-productivity ratio* of the service

$$_x c_k = \frac{c_k}{\varphi_{v_k}}. \quad = \frac{c_k}{MP_k}$$

Now it is evident that the substitution of one service for another service along a particular isoquant will take place as long as the cost-productivity ratio of the former service is smaller than the cost-productivity ratio of the latter. Or expressed in a different way, as long as the marginal productivity of a service in relation to other services is relatively larger than its marginal unit cost, it is profitable to substitute this service for other productive services. In the case of only two services, v_1 and v_2, for example, v_1 will be substituted for v_2 as long as

$$\frac{\varphi_{v_1}}{\varphi_{v_2}} > \frac{c_1}{c_2}$$

and vice versa. The minimum cost combination for a given output is thus obtained when the marginal unit costs of the different productive services are proportional to the marginal productivities of the services; that is, when the cost-productivity ratios of the different services are equal.

(1)
$$c_1 : \ldots \ldots : c_n = \varphi_{v_1} : \ldots \ldots : \varphi_{v_n}$$
$$_x c_1 = \ldots \ldots = {}_x c_n$$

This is a necessary but not a sufficient condition for cost minimum.

2. *The isocosts and the expansion path.* — In the case of a production which uses only two variable productive services we may illustrate graphically the minimum cost conditions for a given output. On a diagram similar to that used in the preceding chapter, we combine with curves, *isocosts*, all service combinations that have the same costs.

34

Thus we obtain a new system of curves as indicated in fig. 8. Since the costs for the fixed services are the same for all service combinations, the isocosts may be defined in relation to the costs of the variable services only.

If now for a particular output we vary the productive services along the given isoquant, the minimum cost combination is evidently reached at the point where the isoquant is tangent to the "lowest possible" isocost. The first of these two conditions, that the isoquant shall be tangent to an isocost, we may express by a general equation; the second condition, that when there are several tangent points between an isoquant and the system of isocosts the lowest isocost yields the minimum cost, must be examined in every particular case. The tangent of an isoquant, according to our earlier analysis, is equal to the relationship between the marginal productivities of the two services

$$\frac{dv_2}{dv_1} = -\frac{\varphi_{v_1}}{\varphi_{v_2}}.$$

The tangent of an isocost is obtained from the condition that the costs are constant. Its properties will depend on the price conditions of the productive services.

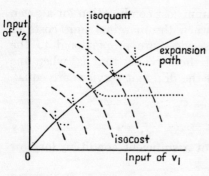

Fig. 8.

If we combine the points of minimum cost for different outputs we obtain a curve which will indicate the most favourable input adjustment for every adjustment in the output (see fig. 8). Following Frisch, we shall call this curve the *expansion path*.[1] For any output of product the firm will always try to substitute the different productive services along the isoquant

---

[1] Frisch, "Tekniske og økonomiske Produktivitetslover", *op. cit.* § 675.

until the expansion path is reached, and for any variation in output it will try to adjust the input along the expansion path.[1] For any point on the expansion path the conditions stated in equation (1) hold true.

We shall now examine the properties of the expansion path as related to the different supply conditions of the productive services examined above. We shall start with the simplest case: when the service prices are given as fixed to the firm. When this task is finished, we shall proceed to the case of continuously variable service prices and, finally, we shall examine the effect on the expansion path of irregular price changes. For each case we shall consider the two conditions of cost minimum: 1) that the isoquant and the isocost must always be tangent to each other; 2) that the tangent point must lie on the "lowest possible" isocost.

3. *The expansion path in the case of fixed service prices*. In a production using only two substitutional services, v_1 and v_2, whose prices are *fixed*, we write the equation for the isocost

$$q_1 v_1 + q_2 v_2 = \text{constant.}$$

where as before, the q's and the v's stand for the prices and the quantities of the services. By differentiation of this equation we get the tangent of the isocost equal to

$$\frac{dv_2}{dv_1} = -\frac{q_1}{q_2}.$$

That is, the isocosts are straight and parallel lines with a negative slope equal to the relationship between the given service prices. On the expansion path, therefore, where the slopes of the isoquants and the isocosts are equal, we

---

[1] Cf. Edgeworth, "The Laws of Increasing and Diminishing Returns", *op. cit.* p. 77: "The property of plural factors which has been pointed out, that in starting from any point (system of factors) there is a choice of directions, is connected with the property that in moving from any initial point to the position of maximum, there is a choice of paths. By the purely mathematical economist the free path would be conceived as movement in that direction by which the greatest increment of profit is continually obtained, the *line of preference* (perpendicular to the line of indifference)."

have the well-known condition that the marginal productivities of the productive services are proportional to the service prices, which in this case are the same as the marginal unit costs

$$\frac{\varphi_{v_1}}{\varphi_{v_2}} = \frac{q_1}{q_2}.$$

For a production using n variable services we have the more general relationship

$$(1\ a) \qquad \varphi_{v_1} : \varphi_{v_2} : \ldots : \varphi_{v_n} = q_1 : q_2 : \ldots : q_n$$

which can be directly obtained from equation (1) by a substitution of the service prices for the marginal unit costs.

Since the isocosts are straight lines, the number of tangent points between an isoquant and the system of isocosts will depend exclusively on the shape of the isoquant. If this is assumed to be a continuous curve without points of inflection as in fig. 6 and fig. 8, there will be only one point of tangency and only one service combination of costs which are minimum for a given output. From the hypothesis that the service prices remain constant irrespective of the input, it follows that the marginal productivities must remain in constant relation throughout the expansion path. We have, however, defined a curve which connects service combinations of constant marginal productivity relation as an isocline. The expansion path is therefore the isocline for which the relationship between the marginal productivities is equal to the relationship between the service prices.

The range of isoclines that can possibly be used as expansion paths must evidently lie inside or on the borderline of the area inside which the marginal productivities of all the services are positive. But it is only when its price is zero that a productive service will be utilized to such an extent that its marginal productivity becomes zero.

4. *The expansion path in the case of continuously variable service prices.* — For the sake of simplicity let us also in this case consider a production with only two variable services. The price of one of these services, q_1, we shall again

assume as fixed, while the price of the other, q_2, is a continuous function of the service quantity,

$$q_2 = q_2 (v_2).$$

The equation for the isocost is the same as before

$$q_1 v_1 + q_2 v_2 = \text{constant};$$

but when we differentiate this equation we must treat the service price, q_2, as a variable

$$q_1 dv_1 + q_2 dv_2 + v_2 dq_2 = 0.$$

Consequently we get a new expression for the tangent of the isoquant

$$\frac{dv_2}{dv_1} = - \frac{q_1}{q_2 + v_2 \dfrac{dq_2}{dv_2}}$$

$$= - \frac{q_1}{q_2 (1 + \lambda_2)}$$

where λ_2 is the price flexibility of the service v_2. The marginal unit cost of the service v_1 is once more equal to its price, but the marginal unit cost of v_2 is equal to the price of this service multiplied by one plus the price flexibility.

Since the tangent of the isocost will vary with one of the service prices, the isocosts will no longer be straight lines but concentric curves which are concave or convex to the axes according as the second derivative $\dfrac{d^2 v_2}{dv_1^2}$ is negative or positive. We therefore have to examine the nature of this derivative. From the equation of the isocost tangent we obtain

$$\frac{d^2 v_2}{dv_1^2} = \frac{q_1 \dfrac{d}{dv_2} \left[q_2 (1 + \lambda_2) \right] \dfrac{dv_2}{dv_1}}{[q_2 (1 + \lambda_2)]^2}$$

$$= - \xi \frac{dc_2}{dv_2}$$

where c_2 is the marginal unit cost of the service v_2

$$c_2 = q_2 (1 + \lambda_2)$$

and

$$\xi = \frac{q_1{}^2}{[q_2 (1 + \lambda_2)]^3}.$$

But since we may expect λ_2 always to be greater than minus one, ξ must be a positive quantity,[1] and we have only to determine the derivative of the marginal unit cost. This derivative we write

$$\frac{dc_2}{dv_2} = \frac{d}{dv_2}\left[q_2 (1 + \lambda_2) \right]$$

$$= 2 \frac{dq_2}{dv_2} + v_2 \frac{d^2 q_2}{dv_2{}^2}.$$

The isoquant pattern, consequently, will depend on the first and the second derivatives of the price function.

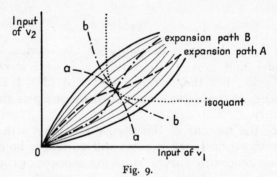

Fig. 9.

When the price, q_2, is an increasing function of the service quantity, we generally expect the price to increase at an increasing rate; i. e. we expect both the first and the second derivatives of the price function to be positive. Under such conditions the derivative of the marginal unit cost must be positive; the second isocost derivative $\frac{d^2 v_2}{dv_1{}^2}$, negative; and the isocosts must be curves concave to the axes (see a—a, fig. 9) If, as before, we assume the

[1] Compare p. 31, above.

isoquants always to be convex, there can exist only one tangent point between the isocost and the system of iso-quants; i. e. the minimum cost combinations are uniquely determined. When, on the other hand, the service price is a decreasing function of the amount bought, we generally expect the price to fall at a decreasing rate; i. e. we expect the second derivative to be positive. In such a case the derivative of the marginal unit cost may be either positive or negative, depending on the relative values of the price derivatives; that is, the relationship between the rate of change in the actual unit price on the one hand, and the change in the amount of savings on the total purchase on the other. When it is positive, the situation is similar to the one just examined; when it is negative, the second isocost derivative $\dfrac{d^2 v_2}{d v_1{}^2}$ is positive, and the isocosts are curves convex to the axes (see b—b, fig. 9). Because of this convexity there may exist a range of tangent points be-tween the isocosts and the isoquants having the expansion path undetermined inside certain limits.

From the equation for the isocost tangent we obtain the condition of the expansion path

$$\frac{\varphi_{v_1}}{\varphi_{v_2}} = \frac{q_1}{q_2\,(\mathrm{I} + \lambda_2)}\,.$$

Like the isocosts, the expansion path will depend on the variation in the marginal unit cost of the service that has a changing price. This cost, we have found, may be ex-pected to increase when the service price is increasing, but it may either increase or decrease in the case of a falling service price. Consequently, if we compare the present situation with that when the prices were fixed for both the services, we find that the constant price service will be more and more substituted for the other service, v_2, when this service increases in price. The expansion path will pass from higher to lower isoclines on its way through the diagram (path A, fig. 9). When, on the other hand, the service, v_2, decreases in price, this service may be substituted for the constant price service and the expansion path may pass from lower to higher isoclines (path B, fig. 9); but the reverse is also possible. If the price function is of such a character that the marginal unit cost of the service increases in spite of the fact that the unit price is falling, we get the rather paradoxical situation where a service with constant price is substituted for another service whose price is falling. The reason is, of course, that it is the relative marginal unit costs and not the relative prices taken by themselves that determine the service substitution.

If the prices of both the services change with their inputs, or if in a production many different services, each one with its separate price function, are used, the character of the expansion path will depend on the relationships between these price functions.

(1 b) $\varphi_{v_1} : \ldots : \varphi_{v_n} = q_1 (1 + \lambda_1) : \ldots : q_n (1 + \lambda_n).$[1]

5. *The influence on the expansion path of irregular price changes.* — The influence of irregular price changes on

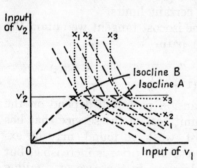

Fig. 10.

the pattern of the isocosts and on the expansion path may be illustrated by a simple example. As before, let us consider a two-service production. The price of one of the services, q_1, we shall assume is fixed irrespective of the quantity bought, while the price of the other service, q_2', remains constant only until the input v_2' is reached. When the firm purchases more than this quantity the price is lowered from q_2' to q_2''. The effect of this price change is illustrated in fig. 10. For inputs of v_2 both smaller and larger than v_2' the isocosts will be straight lines, but at this particular input there will be a break in the lines. Because of the price fall the whole system of isocosts will have a

---

[1] Cf. Schneider, *Theorie der Produktion, op. cit.* pp. 58—59.

rightward shift and the slope of the individual lines will be steeper. The isoquants, which are assumed to be of the same simple character as in the preceding case, will have tangent points with the lower part of the isocost system for all outputs less than x_3, and with the upper part of the system for outputs greater than x_1. For outputs between x_1 and x_3 the individual isoquants will be tangential to the isocost system at two points. Inside this range, therefore, the minimum cost combinations must be determined by our second criterium of the expansion path: the tangent point must lie on the "lowest possible" isocost. In the case illustrated these tangent points are found on the lower part of the isocost system until the output x_2 is reached, and on the upper part for outputs equal to and greater than x_2. The expansion path will consequently at first coincide with the isocline A, fig. 10

$$\frac{\varphi_{v_1}}{\varphi_{v_2}} = \frac{q_1}{q_2'}$$

and later with the isocline B, fig. 10

$$\frac{\varphi_{v_1}}{\varphi_{v_2}} = \frac{q_1}{q_2''}.$$

At the shifting point, the output x_2, there exist two different service combinations of equal minimum cost: one utilizing the service v_2 inside its lower, the other inside its higher price range. Such a situation is, however, far from general; in the case of a more substantial price change the lowest cost combinations may be found on the upper part of the isocost system already at the output x_1.

The Relationship between Costs and Output.

After this discussion of the minimum cost combinations we may proceed to an examination of the relationship between costs and output. Assuming the expansion path as given, we want to study the interdependence of the firm's costs and its output of finished products. To facilitate our study we shall distinguish between several different classes of costs which we shall first define.

1. *Classification of the costs.* — In our technical analysis we have distinguished between fixed and variable productive services. We have observed that the fixed services or the plant remained the same when the output varied within certain given limits, and that it was the existence of these services that was one of the causes of a variable proportional return. Like other productive services the fixed services are assumed to be bought at the beginning of the production period, and to be fully used up at the period's end. The money outlays for these purchases, consequently, are a part of the production cost, a cost that is fixed as long as the output remains within the limits of the plant. This cost, which is characteristically referred to by Schmalenbach as a preparedness cost of production ("Produktionsbereitschaftskosten")[1], we shall name simply the *fixed cost* of the output (C_F).

The money outlays for the variable productive services used in production of a particular output we shall similarly classify as the *variable cost* of the output (C_V). The variable cost is obtained as the sum of the variable services measured in physical units, multiplied by their respective prices. When a physical unit of a service is composed of a fixed proportion of different services,[2] its unit price is calculated from the different price functions of these services. The sum of the fixed and the variable cost is evidently equal to the *total cost* of production (C_T) during the period in question.

In addition to these cost classes we shall use the concepts of average and marginal costs. The *average variable cost* (C_{AV}) is equal to the variable cost divided by the quantity of output, and the *average total cost* (C_{AT}) is equal to the total cost divided by the same quantity. The *marginal cost* (C_M) we shall define as the addition to the total cost caused by a unit increase of the output. Since the fixed cost, by definition, is constant, the marginal cost is obtained by differentiation either of the total cost or of the variable cost

---

[1] E. Schmalenbach, *Der Kontenrahmen* (Leipzig, 1927) p. 31.
[2] Compare p. 12, above.

$$C_M = \frac{dC_T}{dx} = \frac{dC_V}{dx}.$$

From the definitions of the marginal cost, the average variable cost and the average total cost, it follows: (1) that the marginal cost will be less than the average variable cost and the average total cost respectively, until these costs have reached their respective minimum points; (2) that at these minimum points the marginal cost and the average variable or the average total cost will be equal; and (3) that after the minimum points are passed the marginal cost will exceed the average variable cost and average total cost respectively.[1] In the following we shall primarily be concerned with the three cost classes: the marginal, the average variable and the variable costs. When these costs are known for different outputs, and the fixed cost is given, the total and the average total costs are easily obtained.

Similarly to the price flexibility which measured the relative variation of the price of a productive service, we may form the concept of cost flexibility as a measurement of the relative change of the different classes of costs here introduced. The cost flexibility, consequently, we

---

[1] The average variable cost reaches its minimum point when its first derivative is equal to zero and its second derivative is positive. That is, when

$$\frac{dC_{AV}}{dx} = \frac{x \dfrac{dC_V}{dx} - C_V}{x^2} = 0$$

or

$$\frac{dC_V}{dx} = \frac{C_V}{x} = C_{AV}$$

and when

$$\frac{d^2C_{AV}}{dx^2} = \frac{d^2C_V}{dx^2} \frac{1}{x} < 0.$$

Thus, at the minimum point of C_{AV} this cost is equal to $\dfrac{dC_V}{dx}$, and $\dfrac{dC_V}{dx}$ is increasing. Similarly, at the minimum point of the average total cost, this cost is equal to $\dfrac{dC_V}{dx}$, and $\dfrac{dC_V}{dx}$ is increasing. For a fuller discussion of these relationships and their geometrical representation see, for example, Amoroso, "La curva statica di offerta", *Giornale degli Economisti*, LXX, 1930, pp. 5 f., H. Stackelberg, *Grundlagen einer reinen Kostentheorie* (Vienna, 1932) pp. 25 ff. and Robinson, *Economics of Imperfect Competition*, pp. 26—43.

define as the relative cost variation divided by the relative variation of output.[1]

$$\lambda_C = \frac{dC}{dx} : \frac{dx}{x} = \frac{dC}{dx} \cdot \frac{x}{C}.$$

It can easily be shown that the flexibility of the average variable cost is always equal to the flexibility of the variable cost minus one.

2. *The relationship between costs and output when the service prices are fixed.* — Let us now examine how these different classes of costs are affected by changes in the quantity of output, and start out with the assumption that the service prices are fixed. The variable cost, evidently, is equal to the sum of the quantities of the services multiplied by their respective prices

$$C_V = \Sigma q_k v_k$$
$$k = 1, \ldots, n.$$

and the marginal cost is equal to the derivative of this sum

$$\frac{dC_V}{dx} = \frac{\Sigma q_k dv_k}{dx}.$$

But under the conditions assumed, the price of a service, q_k, represents the marginal unit cost of this service, and this cost is equal to the cost-productivity ratio of the service multiplied by its marginal productivity

$$q_k = {}_x c_k \varphi_{v_k}.\,[2]$$

Since the cost-productivity ratios of the different services on the expansion path are the same, we can write the marginal cost

$$\frac{dC_V}{dx} = {}_x c_k \frac{\Sigma \varphi_{v_k} dv_k}{dx}.$$

---

[1] The same relation is referred to by Schneider as the "cost elasticity" (*Theorie der Produktion*, pp. 34—35). Since the term elasticity generally signifies the relationship between the relative change of a quantity and the relative change of a price, we have here avoided the term, and instead have used the term flexibility, which refers to the reverse relationship. Moore and Schultz refer to the same relationship under the name of "relative cost". [Cf. Moore, *Synthetic Economics*, p. 77 and H. Schultz, *Statistical Laws of Demand and Supply* (Chicago, 1928) p. 124.]

[2] See p. 33, above.

or, since the sum of the marginal products, $\Sigma \varphi_{v_k} dv_k$, is equal to dx,

(2) $$C_M = {}_x c_1 = \ldots\ldots = {}_x c_n.$$

That is, on the expansion path the marginal cost of output and the cost-productivity ratios of the different services are equal. This relationship holds true, as we shall see, irrespective of whether the service prices are fixed or variable.

In the special case when the services are always varied in the same proportions, that is, when the expansion path is a straight line starting from the point of origin, the average variable, the variable and the marginal costs stand in a simple relation to one another. If in the expression for the average variable cost

$$C_{AV} = \frac{\Sigma q_k v_k}{x}$$

$$k = 1, \ldots, n.$$

we make a substitution similar to the above, we get

$$C_{AV} = {}_x c_k \frac{\Sigma \varphi_{v_k} v_k}{x}.$$

But when the services are varied in the same proportions, the sum of the quantities of the productive services, each one multiplied by its marginal productivity, is equal to the quantity of output multiplied by the function coefficient.[1] Introducing this relationship into our formula we get

(3) $$\begin{aligned} C_{AV} &= {}_x c_k \cdot \varepsilon \\ &= C_M \cdot \varepsilon. \end{aligned}$$

That is, on the expansion path the average variable cost is equal to the marginal cost multiplied by the function coefficient. It therefore follows that the variable cost must be equal to the product of the marginal cost, the function coefficient and the quantity of output

(4) $$C_V = C_M \cdot \varepsilon \cdot x.$$

[1] Compare p. 17, above.

Thus, as long as the services are changed in the same proportions and the service prices are constant, the cost development on the expansion path is determined solely by the character of the production function. When the function coefficient is greater than unity the average variable cost will exceed, when less than unity fall short of, the marginal cost. Not only the absolute values of the different cost classes are determined by the properties of the function coefficient, but also the flexibilities of the costs.[1] The flexibility of the variable cost is thus equal to the inverse value of the function coefficient

$$\lambda_{C_V} = \frac{dC_V}{dx} \cdot \frac{x}{C_V} = \frac{1}{\varepsilon}$$

the flexibility of the average variable cost is equal to this quantity minus one

$$\lambda_{C_{AV}} = \frac{1}{\varepsilon} - 1$$

and the flexibility of the marginal cost equal to the flexibility of the average variable cost minus the flexibility of the function coefficient itself

$$\lambda_{C_M} = \lambda_{C_{AV}} - \lambda_\varepsilon = \frac{1}{\varepsilon} - 1 - \lambda_\varepsilon$$

where

$$\lambda_\varepsilon = \frac{d\varepsilon}{dx} \cdot \frac{x}{\varepsilon}.$$

If, as in our earlier analysis,[2] we assume that the function coefficient generally decreases with increasing input, the flexibility of the function coefficient will be negative and decreasing. From this assumed knowledge of the properties of the function coefficient, consequently, we may deduce the relationship between the different costs and the output, as is indicated in table I, and fig. II. If, instead, we assume that the production yields constant proportional return, and that, therefore, the function coefficient is unity all

---

[1] Cf. Frisch, *op. cit.* § 677.
[2] See chapter II, pp. 22—23.

Table I.

Technical region ε	Marginal cost		Variable cost		Average variable cost	
	λ_{C_M}	C_M	λ_{C_V}	C_V	$\lambda_{C_{AV}}$	C_{AV}
increasing proportional return $\varepsilon > 1$	at first when $\lambda_\varepsilon > \lambda_{C_{AV}}$ < 0	decreasing	< 1	increasing but at a decreasing rate	< 0	decreasing
	when $\lambda_\varepsilon = \lambda_{C_{AV}}$ 0	reaches minimum value	< 1	increasing: point of inflection	< 0	decreasing
	when $\lambda_\varepsilon < \lambda_{C_{AV}}$ > 0	increasing	< 1	increasing at an increasing rate	< 0	decreasing
constant proportional return $\varepsilon = 1$	> 0	increasing and equal to C_{AV}	1	increasing at an increasing rate	0	reaches minimum value
decreasing proportional return $\varepsilon < 1$	> 0	increasing and $> C_{AV}$	> 1	increasing at an increasing rate	> 0	increasing

along the expansion path — and it is mostly in this case that we actually find proportional service variations — the flexibilities of the marginal and average variable costs will be zero, and these costs will be equal and constant for every output produced.

Also when we leave the assumption of proportional service variations and assume that the services are varied along isoclines of more

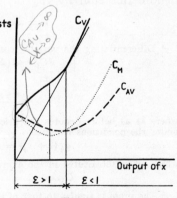

Fig. 11.

or less irregular shape, the different cost relations will be governed solely by the properties of the production function. The connection between the cost aspects and the technical aspects of production can, however, no longer be stated in the same simple mathematical terms, even if the general character of the cost pattern is similar to that already described.

3. *The relationship between costs and output in the case of continuously variable service prices.* — If we change our postulate and assume that the service prices are functions of the quantities of the services bought, we shall still have the marginal cost of output equal to the cost-productivity ratios of the different services.[1] But the relationship between the marginal and the variable costs is more complex than in the case of fixed service prices. If, again, we assume that the productive services are changed in equal proportions, although the assumption is in this case even less realistic than in the preceding one, we write the variable cost

$$C_V = \Sigma q_k v_k = \Sigma q_k (1 + \lambda_k) v_k - \Sigma q_k v_k \lambda_k.$$

The first of these sums becomes equal to the product of the marginal cost, the function coefficient and the quantity of output

$$\Sigma q_k (1 + \lambda_k) v_k = C_M \cdot \varepsilon \cdot x^2$$

but we have also an additional sum in our equation. Let us denote this sum by Λ

$$\Lambda = \Sigma q_k v_k \lambda_k.$$

___

[1] Differentiating the variable cost we have

$$\frac{dC_V}{dx} = \frac{d(\Sigma q_k v_k)}{dx}$$

$$= \frac{\Sigma q_k (1 + \lambda_k) dv_k}{dx}$$

where λ_k as before denotes the price flexibility of the service v_k. But under the conditions assumed

$$q_k (1 + \lambda_k) = c_k = {}_x c_k \mathcal{P}_{v_k}$$

which when substituted in the expression above, gives us

$$C_M = {}_x c_1 = \ldots = {}_x c_n$$

[2] The proof is similar to that of equation (4), above.

The sign of Λ obviously depends on the sign of the price flexibilities: Λ is positive when the service prices are increasing, and negative when the service prices are decreasing. Introducing this Λ into our equation for the variable cost we get

(4 a) $$C_V = C_M \cdot \varepsilon \cdot x - \Lambda$$

and from this relationship we obtain the average variable cost as

(3 a) $$C_{AV} = C_M \cdot \varepsilon - \frac{\Lambda}{x}.$$

The relationships between the different types of costs no longer depend on the technical conditions only, that is, on the function coefficient, but on the combined effect of these conditions and the supply conditions of the productive services which determine the properties of the factor Λ. When the service prices are fixed and the price flexibilities are consequently zero, Λ vanishes from our equations, and we obtain the same relationships as in equations (3) and (4) above.

The flexibilities of the different classes of costs are also determined by the same sets of conditions: the technical conditions characterized by the function coefficient, and the supply conditions of productive services characterized by the factor Λ. Thus, the flexibility of the variable cost becomes

$$\lambda_{C_V} = \frac{\mathrm{I}}{\varepsilon} + \frac{\Lambda}{C_V \varepsilon};$$

and the flexibility of the average variable cost

$$\lambda_{C_{AV}} = \frac{\mathrm{I}}{\varepsilon} + \frac{\Lambda}{C_V \varepsilon} - \mathrm{I}.\,[1]$$

all under the explicit assumption of proportional service variations. If the service prices are increasing functions of the quantities bought, and Λ is thus positive, the flexi-

---

[1] The flexibility of the marginal cost will depend on the derivative of Λ with respect to x, which in its turn is determined by the properties of the price flexibilities. But we shall not enter into these relationships here.

bilities of the variable and average variable costs become relatively greater than they would be if the service prices were fixed, and the average variable cost reaches its minimum point at a relatively earlier stage (see curves C_V' and C_{AV}', fig. 12). If, on the other hand, the service prices are decreasing functions of the service quantities, the two cost flexibilities are relatively smaller than in the case of fixed service prices, and the minimum average variable cost is reached at a relatively later stage[1] (see curves C_V'' and C_{AV}'', fig. 12).

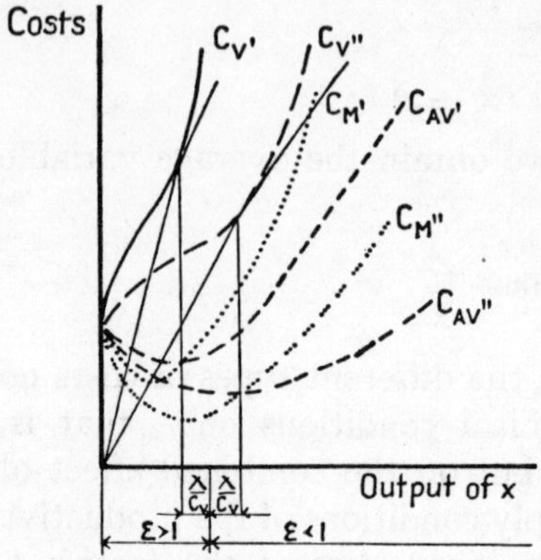

Fig. 12.

These main characteristics of the cost curves in the case of continuously variable service prices and the general relationship between these cost curves and the cost curves when the service prices are fixed, will remain fundamentally the same, also when we leave the assumption of proportional service variations. But instead of definite and simple formulas of the different costs and cost flexibilities we get mathematical functions of a more general type.

4. *The relationship between costs and output when the productive services have irregular price changes.* — For the

---

[1] The average variable cost is at a minimum when its flexibility is zero. In the case of constant service prices this condition is fulfilled when

$$\frac{1}{\varepsilon} - 1 = 0$$

or when

$$\varepsilon = 1.$$

In the present case the minimum cost condition is fulfilled when

$$\frac{1}{\varepsilon} + \frac{\Delta}{C_V \varepsilon} - 1 = 0$$

or when

$$\varepsilon = 1 + \frac{\Delta}{C_V}.$$

Therefore, when Δ is positive ε is greater, and when Δ is negative ε is smaller, than unity.

study of the relationship between costs and output when the productive services have irregular price changes let us return to the simple example described on pages 40 and 41 above and illustrated in fig. 10. We assumed there a production in which only two variable services are used, v_1 and v_2. The price of v_1 is fixed at q_1; the price of v_2 remains at the level q_2' until the quantity v_2' of the service is bought. When this quantity or more is taken the price is lowered to q_2''. This price change, it will be remembered, produces at the output x_2 a sudden shift of the expansion path from a "lower" to a "higher" isocline. The relationship between costs and output on the expansion path is consequently equal to the relationship between costs and output on the lower isocline (A, fig. 10) till the output reaches the quantity x_2, and from that point on is equal to the same relationship on the higher isocline (B, fig. 10).

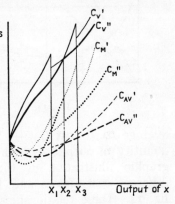

Fig. 13.

We have illustrated these relationships between costs and output on the two isoclines and on the expansion path in fig. 13. If we observe the lower isocline we find that the three costs C_V', C_{AV}' and C_M' develop in a regular fashion till the output x_3 is reached. At this point all three cost curves show a sudden shift downwards. After the shift they again develop regularly. On the upper isocline (the costs C_V'', C_{AV}'' and C_M'') we find the same phenomena, except that the shift here occurs at the lower output x_1. The costs on the higher isocline exceed at the beginning the costs on the lower isocline. The shift at x_1 decreases the marginal cost C_M'' below C_M'. The variable and average variable costs, C_V'' and C_{AV}'', however, fall short of C_V' and C_{AV}' only for outputs greater than x_2. On the expansion path the variable and average variable costs are uninterruptedly increasing, but their flexibilities show a discontinuous change at the output x_2, where also the marginal cost has a sudden shift. In the case of a more substantial price change, however, not only the marginal but also the variable and average variable costs may have abrupt changes, which would then occur at the output x_1.

5. *The total and the average total costs.* Having established the relationship between variable cost and output, we get the total cost of production, C_T, merely by an addition of the fixed cost, C_F. Similarly, the average total cost C_{AT} is obtained as the sum of the average fixed cost C_{AF} — the fixed cost divided by the quantity of output — and the average variable cost. A graphic illustration of the relationship between these different cost classes and the marginal cost is given in fig. 14. These relationships are familiar to all students of economics and deserve but few comments here.[1] We may merely repeat that the marginal cost, which is influenced by changes in the variable cost only, intersects the average variable cost as well as the average total cost in their respective minimum points.[2] The minimum point of the average total cost is consequently reached at a later stage of output expansion than the minimum point of the average variable cost.

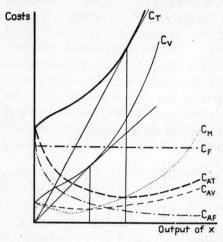

Fig. 14.

---

[1] For an extensive analysis of these relationships, see Stackelberg, *Kostentheorie, op. cit.* pp. 20—36 and 94—99.

[2] See p. 43, above, n. 1.

CHAPTER IV.

THE RATE OF RETURN AND THE MAXIMIZA-
TION PROBLEM.

The aim of the business firm's activity, we have assumed, is to maximize the net return on its capital; and it will manage its production accordingly. Our task is to examine the different forces influencing the entrepreneur in his production management and to discover the principles on which those forces operate. It will be remembered that we have classified the forces in four different groups, of which two, the technical conditions of production and the supply of productive services, have already been the subject of our attention. The remaining two, the demand for the firm's output and the supply of capital funds, will be examined in the present chapter. At first we shall study these forces separately, and later relate them to the other production determining forces, and discuss the maximization problem in full.

THE DEMAND FOR THE FIRM'S OUTPUT.

1. *Demand expectations.* — The demand for the firm's output may be represented analogously to the supply of a productive service by a series of price-quantity combinations. For every quantity of output the firm offers on the market there is a corresponding definite price; and for every price the firm charges, a definite quantity of the output will be demanded. The magnitudes of these prices and quantities are determined by a number of circumstances such as the tastes and incomes of the buyers, the competition from other producers and the sales organization of the business firm. At any particular moment when all

these conditions may be assumed as given data, the relationship between the quantity sold and the price obtained is uniquely determined.

But it is not the actual demand for the firm's output at the end of the time period that determines the production process. The firm's production requires time and must be planned in advance. It is, therefore, the entrepreneur's anticipation of the future demand at the time when the production plans are made that is important. How these anticipations are formed does not interest us here; it is certain, however, that market experience from earlier periods and knowledge of general business conditions and competitive conditions in the firm's particular field are important factors. Here we need only assume that the entrepreneur has a definite pattern of response to his various indefinite demand expectations.[1]

We may simplify our analysis of the demand by assuming that the time required for the sale of the firm's output is negligible. Let us say that the output is sold on the very last day of the time period. This assumption enables us to disregard all the problems of sales and price relations between different dates in time. Such questions as the effect of the firm's present output or price on the future actions of other producers or on the future behaviour of the buyers are thus eliminated. They will be taken up for examination in our study of the poly-periodic production.

2. *The demand function.* — The quantitative relationship between anticipated outputs and anticipated prices may be illustrated graphically. In fig. 15 and fig. 16 the abscissae of the diagrams represent the quantity of output and the ordinates the price. We shall disregard the possibility of a price discrimination on the selling market, and assume

---

[1] Cf. J. M. Keynes, *The General Theory of Employment, Interest and Money* (New York, 1936) p. 24, n. 3: "An entrepreneur, who has to reach a practical decision as to his scale of production, does not, of course, entertain a single undoubting expectation of what the sale-proceeds of a given output will be, but several hypothetical expectations held with varying degrees of probability and definiteness. By his expectation of proceeds I mean, therefore, that expectation of proceeds which, if it were held with certainty, would lead to the same behaviour as does the bundle of vague and more various possibilities which actually makes up his state of expectation when he reaches his decision."

that the price represents the price which the firm expects actually to get for its product.[1]

The use of a simple curve (a demand curve) to express the relationship between the anticipated prices and quantities implies that the firm bases its calculations on the assumption of a definite price for every quantity of output to be sold. It may be true that the entrepreneur actually anticipates only one price, or, what is more plausible, that he anticipates a series of possible prices for a given output, but that he selects and evaluates one price as the most probable or expected. The calculation process through which the entrepreneur reaches his price estimates does not interest us at the moment; we only assume that for every output there exists one and only one price anticipation.[2]

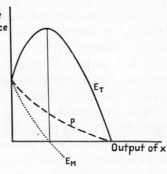

Fig. 15.

As the demand curves are drawn in fig. 15 and fig. 16, there is but one output which corresponds to every price and one price which corresponds to every output. An increase in sales is always followed by a decline in price. This simple relationship, which may be observed generally in practical life, permits us to express one of the two variables, price and quantity, as a unique and single-valued function of the other. We may choose either the price or the quantity as the independent variable. That is, the result will be the same if the firm fixes its output

---

[1] For an analysis of price discrimination problems the reader must be referred to other sources, for example Joan Robinson, *Economics of Imperfect Competition op. cit.*, Ch. 15.

[2] For a discussion of the relationship between the single-valued anticipations and the more vague price expectations of the firm, compare G. Myrdal, *Prisbildningsproblemet och föränderligheten* (Uppsala, 1927) chapters VI—X, J. R. Hicks, "The Theory of Uncertainty and Profit", *Economica*, 1931, pp. 170—89, and A. Hart, "Anticipations, Business Planning and the Cycle", Unpublished doctor's thesis, Department of Economics, University of Chicago, 1936, Chapter IV.

at a certain quantity and lets the market determine the price, or if it fixes the price and lets the market determine the quantity. In the following treatment we shall choose to express the commodity price (p) as a function of the output (x). We, therefore, write our *demand function*

$$p = p(x).[1]$$

3. *Total revenue and marginal revenue.* — The expected price at a certain output represents also the expected *average revenue* to the firm at that output. On analogy with our earlier development of different cost concepts, we may now develop the concepts of total and marginal revenue from the concept of average revenue. The *total revenue* of output (E_T, fig. 15) is, then, the product of the unit price and the quantity of output sold. In the case of the demand curves here assumed, the total revenue can be expressed as a unique and single value function of the output.

$$E_T = x \cdot p = x \cdot p(x).$$

The *marginal revenue* of output expresses the increase in the total revenue produced by a unit increment in the quantity sold. Its mathematical formulation is obtained by differentiation of the equation above:

$$E_M = p + x \frac{dp}{dx}.$$

If we introduce the concept of price flexibility, which has already been defined as the quotient of the relative price and the relative quantity changes,

$$\lambda_p = \frac{dp}{p} : \frac{dx}{x} = \frac{dp}{dx} \cdot \frac{x}{p}$$

the marginal revenue may be written

$$E_M = p \left(1 + \frac{dp}{dx} \frac{x}{p} \right) = p(1 + \lambda_p).$$

---

[1] We shall assume this demand function as a given datum for our analysis, and disregard the possibility that the firm may influence the price or the quantity sold by different means of sales promotion.

That is, the increase of the total revenue caused by a unit increment of the output is equal to the price multiplied by one plus the price flexibility.

In accordance with our assumption of a negatively sloping demand curve the price flexibility must be a negative number. A possible exception to this condition exists in the case where the firm can sell unlimited quantities at a constant price (i. e. where the demand curve is horizontal), when the price flexibility is zero and the marginal revenue is equal to the price. Under other circumstances the marginal revenue is less than the price. When the price flexibility is greater than minus one, the marginal revenue is positive; when it is smaller than minus one, the marginal revenue is negative. The relationship between price flexibility and marginal revenue is shown in the first two columns of table II.

Table II.

Price flexibility p	Marginal revenue E_M	Total revenue E_T
o	positive constant, equal to p	increasing proportional to output
> -1	positive, decreasing $p > E_M > 1$	increasing but at a decreasing rate
-1	zero	constant
< -1	negative	decreasing

4. *The price flexibility.* — Let us now study the properties of the price flexibility for two characteristic demand functions. In the most simple case, fig. 15, where the price gradually falls to zero and the demand curve has no points of inflection, the price flexibility will continuously decrease with increasing outputs. Up to the point when it reaches minus one, the marginal revenue is positive, although decreasing, and the total revenue increases. At a price flexibility of minus unity, the marginal revenue is zero and the total revenue constant; it has reached its

maximum and only maximum value. For further increases in the output, the price flexibility declines below minus one, the marginal revenue is negative and the total revenue decreasing. (See table II.)

Often, however, the demand curve may show a less regular appearance and have one or several points of inflection (see curve *p*, fig. 16). The demand conditions may, for instance, be such that a large group of new buyers appears or new kinds of demand develop as soon as the price has

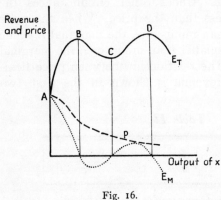

Fig. 16.

reached a certain low level. When such is the case the price flexibility may have consecutive decreases and increases; and the same holds true for the marginal revenue. The total revenue may have points of constancy at several different outputs, some of which are maximum and others minimum points (see fig. 16). Of the different regions of the demand curve which we may distinguish in this case, only those, of course, for which the price flexibility is greater than minus one and the marginal revenue positive are of interest to the entrepreneur. Since the cost of production of an output increment is always positive, the firm has no reason to extend its output to such an extent that the revenue from the increment becomes negative. In fig. 16, for example, it is only those parts of the different revenue curves which lie between A and B, and C and D that have significance for the maximization problem of the firm.

THE SUPPLY OF CAPITAL FUNDS.

1. *Outside investments and borrowed funds.* — To be able to purchase productive services at the beginning of

the production activity and to finance the activity until remuneration for its output is obtained, the business firm must have command over capital funds. There are two possible sources of supply for these funds: the firm's privately owned funds and its borrowed funds. From our assumption that one period's activity is always fully liquidated before the following period's activity commences, it follows that all the firm's capital is in liquid form at the beginning of the period and is thus available to finance new production.

Assume that the total amount of a firm's own funds is fixed at any particular date in time. The amount of capital invested in a certain activity is nevertheless variable, and will depend on the rate of return from that activity as compared with the rate of interest obtainable from other kinds of investments. The capital funds invested outside the particular production under consideration may be classified as *outside investments*, I. When the outside investments increase in amount, the rate of interest obtainable may either remain constant or decrease, depending upon the relative value of the firm's investments to the total value of the investments on the capital market. Let us here assume that the interest rate decreases with an increase in the investments and vice versa; in other words, let us assume that additional investments of the firm have to seek less and less remunerative employment. We shall express the relationship between the rate of interest, i, and the amount of outside investments by a function.

$$i = i\,(I).$$

and assume that this function is unique and single valued.

While at any particular time the firm's own funds may be assumed as fixed in quantity, its *borrowed funds*, L, can be varied through increased or decreased borrowing. The interest rate paid for this borrowing may be constant irrespective of the amount borrowed, be constant inside some definite limits, or may vary more or less continuously. Let us assume that the interest rate increases continuously with the amount of the borrowed funds and, as before, let us express the relationship between the rate of interest, i, and the amount of borrowed funds by a function

$$i = i^{\cdot}(L)$$

which we also assume is unique and single valued. But while the derivative of the investment function above is assumed to be negative, the derivative of this function is positive. As in the case of the prices in our earlier supply and demand functions, the interest rates in these functions may be regarded as *average rates* received on the total amount of outside investments or paid on the total amount of borrowed funds. Again we shall disregard the problem of price (interest) discrimination.[1]

2. *The marginal rate of interest.* — Although the average rates of interest on the total amount of outside investments or of borrowed funds are significant for the entrepreneur's calculations, it is even more important for him to know the interest rates obtained on the last increment of the firm's investments, or paid on the last increment of borrowing. These latter rates we shall call the *marginal rates of interest*, i_M. If L is the total amount of borrowing and i is the average rate of interest paid during a unit time period, the total interest cost of the same period is $i\,L$, and the increase of this cost caused by an infinitesimal increment in the amount borrowed, dL, is $d\,(i\,L)$. It is this increase expressed as a rate on the increment dL which constitutes the marginal rate of interest during the unit period

$$i_M = \frac{d\,(i\,L)}{dL}$$

$$= i\,(1 + \lambda_i)$$

_____

[1] The assumption here made of a continuously varying interest rate with regard both to the firm's borrowed funds and its outside investments is much more realistic than, for instance, the assumption of a continuously varying service price. In practical life there exist so many different possibilities for a firm to finance successive increments of production, or to invest successive increments of capital that the changes in the interest rate paid or obtained will in most cases be fairly gradual. The assumption that there exists no price discrimination as regards borrowing and outside investment, on the other hand, corresponds far less to the conditions generally prevailing in actual business life.

where λ_i is the flexibility of the interest rate

$$\lambda_i = \frac{di}{dL}\frac{L}{i}.$$

In the case of outside investments we have a similar expression for the marginal rate of interest, but then, of course, the interest flexibility

$$\lambda_i = \frac{di}{dI}\frac{I}{i}$$

is derived from the average investment rate and not from the borrowing rate. In both cases it follows that when the average rate of interest is constant and consequently the interest flexibility is zero, the marginal and the average rates of interest are the same. Under other circumstances, the marginal rate is assumed to exceed the average rate when the firm borrows, and to fall short of the average rate when the firm invests capital funds.

THE RATE OF RETURN AND THE MAXIMIZATION PROBLEM.

1. *The net return and the rate of return.* — The *net return* of the firm's activity during a certain period we obtain by subtracting the minimum costs (the costs on the expansion path) of the period from the total revenue obtained. The minimum costs are composed of the total costs of the productive services engaged in production, called simply the total costs in our earlier analysis, and of the total interest costs when borrowed funds are employed. The total revenue is composed of the total revenue of output and of the total interest revenue, if any, obtained from outside investments. The *rate of return* on the firm's capital is obtained by expressing the net return as a rate on the firm's own funds during the period in question.[1]

Let us at first assume that the firm engages borrowed funds in its activity, but that no outside investments occur. Certain investment opportunities, of course, always exist outside the activity in question, but these investment

[1] In Fisher's terminology "the rate of return over cost", cf. Irving Fisher, *Theory of Interest* (New York, 1930), pp. 155 ff.

opportunities are potential only and are not actually used. Under these assumptions the total revenue becomes equal to the total revenue of output, E_T in our earlier notations, and the total cost equal to the total cost of the productive services on the expansion path, C_T, plus the interest cost. If, as before, we denote the total amount of borrowing by L and the average interest rate paid during the unit period by i, these interest costs equal iL. The net return, R, consequently becomes

(1) $$R = E_T - (C_T + iL).$$

Since we are dealing with simple interest, the rate of return, r, may be expressed as a simple rate on the firm's own funds, K, during the unit period

(2) $$r = \frac{R}{K} = \frac{E_T - (C_T + iL)}{K}.$$

It is the maximization of this rate of return which is the goal of the firm's activity. But from our assumption that the firm's own funds are fixed in amount at the time when the production activity commences and that the investment period is also a fixed quantity, it follows that when the rate of return on the firm's capital is maximum, the net return and the value of the firm's capital at the end of the investment period are also maximum. In other words, the maximization of any one of these three magnitudes automatically includes the maximization of the others.

2. *The marginal return and marginal rate of return.* — In addition to these concepts of net return and rate of return on the firm's own funds, which are both related to the firm's total productive activity, we shall introduce two different concepts related to a marginal increment of production. The first of these concepts, the *marginal return*, may be defined as the difference between the increase in the firm's total revenue and the increase in its total cost, *exclusive* of interest costs, caused by a unit increment in the output.

These increments we have earlier classified as the marginal revenue of output, E_M, and the marginal cost of production, C_M, respectively. The marginal return, R_M, we therefore write

(3) $$R_M = E_M - C_M.$$

The second concept, the *marginal rate of return*, represents the marginal return expressed as a rate on the increment in productive investment required for the unit increase in the output, during the period in question.[1] From our initial assumption that only the productive services have to be paid at the beginning of the production period, while the interest costs are not paid until the revenue of output is received, it follows that this increase in productive investment must be equal to the marginal cost of production. The marginal rate of return, r_M, expressed as a simple rate of increase in the productive investment during the unit period consequently becomes

$$E_M\left(1 - \tfrac{1}{n}\right) = C_M$$

(4) $$r_M = \frac{E_M - C_M}{C_M}.\qquad \frac{1-\left(1-\tfrac{1}{n}\right)}{\left(1-\tfrac{1}{n}\right)} = \frac{\tfrac{1}{n}}{1-\tfrac{1}{n}} = \frac{1}{n-1}$$

3. *The maximization problem.* — In order to determine the output which yields a maximum rate of return on the firm's own capital, a maximum net return and a maximum value of the capital at the end of the period, we merely have to differentiate the rate of return, as written in equation (2), with respect to the output. When this derivative is zero, that is, when changes in output no longer produce additional net returns, and when the second derivative is negative, the maximum rate of return from the production in question is reached. The necessary maximum condition we therefore write

$$\frac{dr}{dx} = \frac{1}{K}\left(\frac{dE_T}{dx} - \frac{dC_T}{dx} - \frac{d(iL)}{dL} \cdot \frac{dL}{dx}\right) = 0.$$

The first and the second expression inside the parentheses we recognize as the marginal revenue and the marginal cost respectively. The derivative $\dfrac{d(iL)}{dL}$ is, by definition,

---

[1] Compare Fisher's "marginal rate of return over cost". *Ibid.*

the same as the marginal rate of interest, and $\dfrac{dL}{dx}$, according to our present assumptions, is equal to the marginal cost of production. With the firm's own funds as constant, we may consequently write the first maximum condition

$$E_M - C_M - C_M \cdot i_M = 0.$$

[handwritten: $MR = C_M(1 + i)$]

This can be expressed in two different forms:

$$\left.\frac{E_M - C_M}{C_M} = i_M\right\}$$

or

[handwritten: $= \dfrac{1}{n-1}$]

$$(5) \qquad\qquad r_M = i_M$$

and

$$(5\ a) \qquad\qquad E_M = C_M\,(1 + i_M).$$

In order to receive a maximum rate of return on its own capital the firm will expend its production to a point where the marginal rate of return equals the marginal rate of interest; or, which amounts to the same thing, to a point where the marginal revenue of output equals the marginal cost, inclusive of interest cost. As long, therefore, as a change in the output may be expected to produce a greater increase in the total revenue than in the total cost, the change will be made. In a mono-periodic production which under unchanged external conditions repeats itself in a series of periods, consequently, the firm may reach the most profitable output step by step, even if the entrepreneur cannot anticipate the full extent of the demand and the cost curves.[1]

The sufficient maximum condition which is obtained when the second derivative of the rate of return with respect to output is negative

$$\frac{d^2 r}{dx^2} = \frac{d^2 E_T}{dx^2} - \frac{d}{dx}\left[\frac{dC_T}{dx}(1 + i_M)\right] < 0$$

---

[1] Under "unchanged external conditions" we include the condition that the time elapsing or the steps chosen for the firm's output adjustment will have no effect on the different demand and cost curves.

is fulfilled when the marginal cost, inclusive of interest cost, increases more rapidly with respect to output than the marginal revenue. That is, when the marginal cost curve intersects the marginal revenue curve from below.

4. *The influence of outside investments.* — It is easily seen that the conditions for a maximum rate of return here developed hold true also in the case when a firm does not employ borrowed funds, but instead engages part of its own capital in outside investments. An increase in current production is in such a case financed by a transfer of funds from the outside investments, and the most profitable output is reached when the marginal interest rate on these investments is equal to the marginal rate of return. In the more complex situation when the firm engages both in borrowing and in lending, the maximum conditions require a simultaneous equality of all the three marginal rates: the marginal interest rate of borrowing and of outside investment and the marginal rate of return.

The existence of actual or potential outside investments has its bearing on the maximum conditions also in another way. In order that the firm shall start a production activity it is, of course, necessary that the maximum rate of return expected shall exceed or at least be equal to the interest rate the firm can obtain if it invests all its capital in outside investments. This condition is independent of those earlier stated. Because of the existence of fixed costs, of different kinds of irregularities in the marginal costs and the marginal revenues of production, it may in some cases be possible for the average rate of return to fall short of the average interest rate in spite of the equality between the marginal rates. If, as before, the firm's own funds are denoted by K, the interest rate obtained if these funds are all invested in outside investments may be written

$$i_o = i\,(K).$$

Taken all together, the conditions for a maximum rate of return on the firm's own funds therefore become

$$\begin{cases} r \geqslant i_o \\ r_M = i_M \\ \dfrac{d^2 r}{d x^2} < 0 . \end{cases}$$

5. *Single and multiple maximum points.* — Let us now examine these maximum conditions with reference to the cost and revenue curves earlier discussed. (*a*) If we have a negatively sloping curve for the marginal revenue, as in fig. 15, and the marginal cost curve, for example the curve C_M in fig. 11 or 12,[1] intersects this curve in the region where the marginal cost is increasing, the intersection point of the two curves represents a maximum point, and the only maximum point existing. In order that the firm shall engage in production, the rate of return at this point must be equal to or exceed the interest rate on potential outside investments. (*b*) If, instead, the marginal revenue curve has several points of inflection, as in fig. 16, or the marginal cost curve is discontinuous because of sudden changes in the interest rate or in the service prices (fig. 13, chapter III), the two curves may have several points of intersection. Of these points only those are maximum points at which the cost curve passes the revenue curve from below; where it passes the revenue curve from above, the rate of return is a minimum. Of the different maximum points, that one is chosen which yields the absolute maximum rate of return, and it is that rate which must exceed or equal the rate of interest on potential outside investments. Since the entrepreneur, however, is often unable to anticipate the firm's cost and revenue curves to their full extent, there is a certain tendency for the firm to remain at any maximum point

---

[1] The cost curves in chapter III, it will be remembered, include only the costs of the productive services. But under the conditions here assumed, the introduction of interest costs does not change the general character of the curves. As long as we assume that the rate of interest is either constant or else a continuous function of the amount borrowed, the interest costs will increase continuously with the output, and may merely be added to the costs of the productive services. If, on the other hand, we assume that the rate of interest makes sudden shifts, these shifts will also appear in the interest costs, and will cause irregular changes in the cost curves.

reached, although a greater rate of return could be obtained by a drastic change in its production plans. The risk involved in a cost decrease depending on a major change of the scale and methods of production, or with a price cut sufficient to create a large new demand, often seems too great to the entrepreneur in comparison with the possible increase in the rate of return. In other cases it may be the traditional price policy of the firm that is the decisive factor in the choice of maximum point. In the Swedish publishing business, for instance, there are some firms that specialize in low priced books which are printed in large editions, while some other firms as a general rule charge high prices and thereby limit their editions.

The Maximum Conditions and the Production Determining Forces.

With the examination of the maximum conditions of the rate of return, our analysis of the mono-periodic production process has come to an end. From given technical conditions and given supply conditions of the productive services we have determined what we have called the expansion path of the firm's production, and from these conditions in combination with given demand conditions for the firm's output and given supply conditions of capital funds we have found what particular output on the expansion path the firm will produce. Before we proceed with our study let us summarize and co-ordinate the main results of this analysis.

1. *Summary of the maximum conditions.* — According to our cost analysis in chapter III, the minimum cost for a certain output — the cost on the expansion path — is obtained when the cost-productivity ratios of the productive services are equal to each other, and equal to the marginal cost of output [equation (2)]

$$_xc_1 = {}_xc_2 = \ldots . {}_xc_n = C_M.$$

This equality was actually shown to hold true with regard to the service costs only, but under our present assumptions it will also hold if interest costs are included. The interest costs represent merely a proportional increase in the different elements concerned.

The marginal revenue of the firm is defined as the increase in the total revenue produced by a unit increment of output

$$E_M = p\,(\mathrm{I} + \lambda_p)$$

and we have observed that when the rate of return is maximum the marginal revenue equals the marginal cost of production, inclusive of interest cost. Hence we have as a maximum condition for the rate of return that the marginal revenue must be equal to the cost-productivity ratios of the different productive services inclusive of interest costs. Since these latter are by definition equal to the marginal unit costs of the services divided by the respective marginal productivities, we may write

$$p\,(\mathrm{I}+\lambda_p) = \frac{q_1\,(\mathrm{I}+\lambda_1)}{\varphi_{v_1}}\,(\mathrm{I}+i_M) = \ldots = \frac{q_n\,(\mathrm{I}+\lambda_n)}{\varphi_{v_n}}\,(\mathrm{I}+i_M).$$

From this equality it follows that

$$q_1\,(\mathrm{I}+\lambda_1) = \frac{p\,(\mathrm{I}+\lambda_p)\,\varphi_{v_1}}{\mathrm{I}+i_M}$$

$$q_2\,(\mathrm{I}+\lambda_2) = \frac{p\,(\mathrm{I}+\lambda_p)\,\varphi_{v_2}}{\mathrm{I}+i_M}$$

$$\cdots\cdots\cdots\cdots\cdots$$

$$q_n\,(\mathrm{I}+\lambda_n) = \frac{p\,(\mathrm{I}+\lambda_p)\,\varphi_{v_n}}{\mathrm{I}+i_M}.$$

The quantities on the left sides of these equations we recognize as the marginal unit costs of the productive services and the quantities on the right sides as the *marginal value productivities* of the services discounted back to the date of cost payment. We may therefore write as a corollary to our maximization conditions, already established, that in order to obtain a maximum rate of return on its own capital the firm will employ each productive service until its marginal unit cost is equal to the marginal value productivity of the service discounted back to the date of cost payment. In the case of capital funds the marginal unit cost is substituted by the marginal rate of interest, and the marginal value productivity by the marginal rate of return

$$i_M = r_M.$$

When these conditions are fulfilled no change in the scale or in the methods of production will increase the rate of return.[1]

2. *The effect of changes in the production determining forces.* — Using what Schumpeter calls the "principle of variation",[2] we shall now examine the effect of isolated changes in the production determining forces upon the firm's production and rate of return. We may notice that while the volume of production and the use of the different productive services are governed by the relationship between the marginal revenue and the marginal costs, the rate of return is governed by the relationship between the total revenue and the total cost. In order to determine the influence of a certain change on the volume of production and the employment of the different services we therefore have to examine its effect on the marginal cost or the marginal revenue; and in order to determine the influence on the rate of return we have to examine its effect on the total revenue and the total cost. We shall start with

(a) *the technical conditions of production.*

An increase in the technical efficiency of a variable productive service means an increase in its marginal productivity and a decrease in its cost-productivity ratio. But on the expansion path the cost-productivity ratios of the different services must be equal. If the efficiency of

[1] We may notice the difference between the corollary here stated and the conditions determining the expansion path examined on page 33. As long as we were concerned only with the choice of productive services, i. e. with the methods of production, the necessary requirements were limited to the proportionality between the marginal (technical) productivities and the marginal unit costs, but they said nothing about the equality between these different elements. Not until we consider how much to produce with given technical methods does the condition of an equality between the discounted value productivities and the marginal unit costs come in.

[2] Joseph Schumpeter, *Das Wesen und der Hauptinhalt der theoretischen Nationalökonomie* (Leipzig, 1908), pp. 441 ff.

one service increases, this service will therefore be substituted for other services until the equality of the cost-productivity ratios is re-established. An increased efficiency of a variable service will also mean a decrease in the marginal and total costs, an increase in the volume of production and in the rate of return. A decrease in the efficiency of a variable service will have the opposite effect. When it is a fixed service that has increased or decreased in efficiency the result will be very much the same. A more efficient plant will cause the output of the variable services to rise, which for a given volume of production means a lower total cost and an increased rate of return. It will also — at least for a certain range of outputs — cause the marginal productivity of the variable services to increase. Since this increase may vary in extent as between different services, certain adjustments of the expansion path may follow also here, but not necessarily.[1]

(b) *The supply conditions of the productive services.*

When we analyze the effect on the firm's production of changing supply conditions of the productive services, we must again distinguish between fixed and variable services. If it is a fixed productive service that changes in price this change will result in altered total costs and a corresponding change in the rate of return, but it will have no effect on the marginal costs, the expansion path chosen or the quantity of output. Changing supply conditions of a variable service will influence the marginal cost of the service and the marginal and total costs of output. It will thus have an effect both on the methods and volume of production and on the rate of return, but these effects may be different in magnitude and direction. We may distinguish between three possible kinds of changes. Firstly, if the change in the service supply means merely a "shift" up-

[1] We have here assumed that the fixed services always remain constant in absolutely given quantities. If, on the other hand, the fixed services can be obtained in certain standard sizes, the increased efficiency may cause the firm to use a smaller size than before. The main result of the change would then be a fall in the fixed costs, while the marginal productivities of the variable services and the marginal costs of production might be unchanged or even decreased and increased respectively.

wards or downwards of the supply curve of the variable service without a change in the slope of the curve, the marginal unit cost of the service will increase or decrease by an amount exactly corresponding to the increase or decrease of the service price.[1] The supply change will therefore influence the service substitution, the volume of production and the rate of return to an equal degree. When the service price is increased the marginal unit cost of the service is increased and this will cause a partial substitution of the service by other now relatively cheaper services.[2] It will also have a decreasing effect on the volume of production, the amount of borrowing and the rate of return. When the service price is decreased, the effects will be reversed.

If, on the other hand, the change in the service supply includes also an increase or a decrease of the slope of the supply curve of a variable service, the marginal unit cost of the service will increase or decrease relatively more than the service price, and the service substitution and the volume of production will be relatively more affected than the rate of return.

If, finally, the supply change is of such a character that small amounts of the service can be bought cheaper than before, while large amounts are more expensive, the price of the service quantity originally bought may have declined while at the same time the marginal unit cost of the service has increased. We have here a change which will influence

---

[1] If originally the marginal unit cost of the service was

$$c_k' = \left(q_k + \frac{dq_k}{dv_k} v_k \right)$$

and the service price changes by an amount Δq_k, while the slope of the supply curve $\frac{dq_k}{dv_k}$ remains the same, the marginal cost of the service becomes

$$c_k'' = \left(q_k + \Delta q_k + \frac{dq_k}{dv_k} v_k \right) = c_k' + \Delta q_k.$$

[2] To measure the degree of this substitution, Robinson and Hicks have introduced the concept of "elasticity of substitution". A discussion of this concept is outside the bounds of the present essay, and the reader must be referred to Robinson, *op. cit.*, pp. 256—257, and J. R. Hicks, *Theory of Wages* (London, 1932), p. 244.

the service substitution and the volume of production in one direction and the rate of return in another. Since the marginal unit cost of the service is increased, the service will be partially substituted by other services and the volume of production will be decreased. On the other hand, since the service price has decreased, the total cost will decrease and the rate of return increase.[1]

(c) *The demand conditions of the firm's output.*

A change in the demand of the firm's output will influence the marginal and the total revenues, and through these revenues it will have an effect on the volume of production and the rate of return. But as in the case of a change in the service supply, these effects may be of different magnitude or in different directions. Again we may distinguish between three different cases. First, if the change in the demand means a shift of the demand curve without a change of its slope, the marginal revenue will change by an amount that corresponds to the price change, and the effect of the demand change on the volume of production and the rate of return will be similar. A shift upwards of the demand curve will produce an increased marginal revenue and an increased volume of production. It will also increase the rate of return. A shift downwards of the demand curve will have the opposite effects.

If, on the other hand, the change of the demand curve includes also an increase or decrease of the slope of the demand curve (measured positively), the marginal revenue will increase or decrease relatively more than the price, and the demand change will have a correspondingly greater effect on the volume of production than on the rate of return. Finally, when the change of the demand means that a small quantity of output can be sold at a higher price than before, while large quantities have fallen in price, we have a situation where the price of the output quantity originally sold may have risen, while simultaneously the marginal revenue has declined. Such a change will therefore have a tendency to decrease the volume of production while

---

[1] For an example of this case, see Robinson, *op. cit.* pp. 222—223.

at the same time the rate of return increases. The reverse effect is obtained when it is the larger outputs that have risen and the small outputs that have fallen in price.

(d) *The supply conditions of capital funds.*

A change in the supply conditions of the capital funds will have the same effect on the marginal and total costs, on the volume of production and on the rate of return as a change in the supply conditions of the productive services. A shift upwards of the supply curve, for example, will mean an increased average and marginal interest rate, a decrease in the volume of production and the rate of return, and when the shift of the curve is associated with an increase of the slope of the curve, the marginal rate of interest and the volume of production will be altered relatively more than the average interest rate and the rate of return. A shift downwards of the curve will have the reverse effects. Unlike the case of a change of the service supply, a change in the supply of capital funds will not under our present mono-periodic assumptions directly effect the substitution relations between the different productive services.

We have here limited our examination to isolated changes of the production determining forces. In practice, the changes of these forces are generally more complex, a change in one frequently being associated with changes in the other forces. Falling service prices or a falling interest rate during the depression period of a business cycle, for example, are generally combined also with a fall in the demand for the firm's output. Or increased competition from other producers may be associated with an increase in the technical efficiency of production. We need only refer to the conditions generally described as "external" economies or diseconomies of production.[1] But with the elementary analysis here developed, we are able also to examine the effects of these more complex changes.

---

[1] These relationships between the technical conditions and the cost conditions of the individual firm on one hand, and the "Industry" as a whole on the other, are most clearly examined by Viner and Pigou. Cf. J. Viner, "Cost Curves and Supply Curves", *Zeitschrift für National-ökonomie*, III (1931), pp. 38—42, and A. C. Pigou, "An Analysis of Supply" *Economic Journal*, XXXVIII (1928), pp. 238—57.

CHAPTER V.

JOINT PRODUCTION AND JOINT COSTS.

So far our analysis has dealt with the most simple type of production activity. By a series of assumptions the analysis has been restricted to a single technical unit, a single "self-contained" time period and a single homogeneous product. We shall now try to widen the scope of our study. In the present chapter we shall leave the assumption of a single product and consider joint production; in a following chapter, we shall similarly abandon the assumption of a single time period.

Two Types of Joint Production.

1. *The setting of our problems*. — The setting for our problems will be largely the same in the present as in the preceding chapters. We shall be dealing with a firm planning the production of a certain closed period; and, again, the unit of planning will be the technical unit. The firm will once more be assumed to borrow the capital funds and buy the productive services necessary for its activity at the beginning of the period, and to sell its output at the period's end. But here we shall assume that the output no longer consists of a single or homogeneous product but is composed of a series of different commodities. We shall, in other words, have joint production, in a wide sense of the term.[1]

---

[1] For a similar use of the term joint production compare F. W. Taussig, *Principles of Economics* (3rd ed. New York, 1927), vol. ii, p. 395: "When any large plant is used for diverse products, the case is so far one of production at joint cost."

Production will here be classified as joint, or not joint, solely with reference to its effect on the production problems of the individual firm. For other than a production analysis, another basis of classification might

Our task is to examine in how far the relationships which we have already established between input and output and between costs, revenues, and output, can be applied also to the case of joint production. To do this, we shall compare the various production problems of joint and simple production. We shall facilitate the comparison by distinguishing two different types of joint production and discuss them separately: (a) joint production with technically fixed proportions of the different products, and (b) joint production with variable proportions of the different products. We shall start with type (a).

2. *Joint production with technically fixed proportions of the products.* — From the point of view of production policy joint production with a fixed proportion of the products presents to the business firm largely the same problems as does the production of a single product. Since the different products are by technical necessity always produced in constant proportions, the constant combination of the products may for purposes of calculation be defined as the unit of output to which the production function and the cost functions may be related. As far as the technical and the cost relations are concerned, there is, therefore, no difference between an analysis of joint production with fixed proportions and an analysis of simple production. In both cases the different relations may be expressed simply as functions of a single homogeneous output quantity.[1] The demand conditions of the output and the maximization problem of production may be similarly treated. In the case of joint production we must distinguish between the demand conditions of the different products, it is true, but once these demand conditions are given we may calculate the price of the combined output unit and the total and marginal

have been more appropriate. Professor Pigou, in a general discussion on railway rates, for example, defines joint production with reference to its effect on a general price equilibrium. ["Railway Rates and Joint Cost", *Quarterly Journal of Economics*, XXVII (1913), p. 535 and pp. 690—91. Compare also *Economics of Welfare* (2nd ed., London, 1924), p. 267.]

[1] Cf. Marco Fanno, *Contributio alla teoria dell'offerta a costi congiunti* (Rome, 1914) pp. 27—28, n. 2.

$C = C(q)$

revenues at different levels of output.[1] With known relationships between cost and output and between revenue and output, the maximum rate of return may be determined in the same way as in the case of simple production.[2] In the pure theory of production, therefore, joint production with fixed product proportions becomes merely a special case of simple production, and can be covered by the same kind of analysis. This similarity between the two types of production does not necessarily imply, however, that they are also similar in other respects; for example, their individual effects on a general price equilibrium are quite different.

3. *Joint production with technically variable proportions of the products.* — It is when we come to the case of joint production with variable proportions between the products that the real differences between joint production and simple production first appear, and it is this production type that in the following we shall designate by the term joint production. When the proportions between the different products varies with different outputs, there is no longer a homogeneous output unit to which the productivities, costs, and revenues of the different services can be related. Nor is it possible to relate these magnitudes separately to the different products and to calculate their individual costs and revenues, since a change in one of the products will generally influence the technical, the cost and the demand relations of the others. This interrelationship between the different products is the characteristic feature of joint production, and will be the subject of the following analysis.

---

[1] Cf. Marshall, *Principles of Economics* (8th. ed. London, 1920) pp. 388—89, n. 3 and Fanno, *op. cit.*, p. 28.

[2] It should be noticed that although one or several of the joint products, *because of the fixed production relations*, may be produced in such quantities that, if fully sold, their expected marginal revenues would become negative, the sale of these products will cease at a point where their expected total revenues become maximum, and the excess quantities will be wasted. As an example one may mention the gold mines of Boliden in Sweden, which besides gold and copper yield arsenic to such an extent that it exceeds the entire world's consumption. The wasting of this arsenic has, in fact, become one of the more serious problems of the company. [Cf. *The Mineral Industry 1936* (New York, 1937) pp. 41—42.]

Joint Production and Joint Costs, an Element-ARY Case.

In order to illustrate the particular features of joint production, we shall examine a production activity of the simplest kind: a firm which in its production uses only two kinds of services, a fixed service, for example a plant of a certain type, and a variable service. As in the previous case, the variable service may be composed of different elements, such as labour and raw materials, but if such is the case, these elements may be assumed to be combined in a constant proportion which may be treated as the single homogeneous service unit. The output of the process consists of two different products which are produced jointly and which are both sold on the market at the end of the period. Our task is to study the technical and the cost relations of this prototype of joint production.

1. *The relationship between input and output.* — Let us start with the relationship between input and output. The input consists of the plant, which is constant, and the variable service, which changes with the amount of output produced; the output consists of the two commodities jointly produced. As in the case of simple production, the output of one of the products will depend on the quantity of input of the variable service, but, in this joint production, it will further depend on the output of the other product. Thus, if we denote the service quantity by v, and the quantities of the two products by x and y, we may write x as a function of v and y

(1 a) $$x = \varphi_{(x)} (v, y)$$

and y as a function of y and x

(1 b) $$y = \varphi_{(y)} (v, x)$$

These functions are our production functions of x and y.

The partial derivative, with respect to v, of one of the products, such as x, gives us the marginal productivity of the service with respect to that product, assuming the quantity of the other product, y, to be constant. Since the plant is regarded as fixed, we may assume that after a certain input is reached, this marginal productivity of the variable service will decline till it finally becomes zero. Beyond this point an increase in the input of the variable service will have no effect on the output as long as the fixed service remains unchanged. The partial derivative of one of the products, for example x, with respect to the other product y, expresses the technical substitution relation between the two products at a given input of v. In the present case of only two independent variables the value of this derivative is the inverse of the partial derivative of y with respect to x, and is negative. That is, an increased quantity of one of the products may be produced from a given service quantity only if the output of the other product decreases.

Since we have a single variable service, it follows that as soon as the quantities of the two products to be produced are given, the minimum amount of the service necessary for their production is also given. We can then write

$$(1\ c) \qquad\qquad v = \psi\,(x,\ y).$$

This service function is related to the two production functions in such a way that if the values of y or x are the same in the different functions, the partial derivatives of v with respect to x and y respectively, which we shall refer to as the *marginal coefficients of production*, are the inverse magnitudes of the marginal productivities of v with respect to x and y.[1] An examination of the properties of the coefficients of production will reveal some of the fundamental characteristics of joint production.

The marginal coefficients of production express the rate of change of the variable service with respect to each of the two separate products. It is assumed that these rates of change vary with the quantities of the products produced in such a way that when x increases while y is constant, or when y increases while x is constant, the marginal production coefficients $\dfrac{\partial v}{\partial x}$ and $\dfrac{\partial v}{\partial y}$ also increase, at least

---

[1] Cf. Pareto, *Manuel, op. cit.*, p. 607, and J. Schumpeter, "Zur Frage der Grenzproduktivität", *Schmollers Jahrbuch*, LI (1927), pp. 676—677.

after a certain minimum quantity of output has been produced. That is, beyond a minimum output the second partial derivatives $\frac{\partial^2 v}{\partial x^2}$ and $\frac{\partial^2 v}{\partial y^2}$ become positive. But the marginal coefficients of production of one product may also vary with a change in the output of the other product, and it is this variation which represents the peculiar characteristics of joint production. In analysing the nature of this variation we shall distinguish between the following possible cases: (a) when an increase of one product causes the marginal coefficient of production of the other product to decrease, that is, when the mixed derivative $\frac{\partial^2 v}{\partial x\, \partial y}$ is negative, we shall say that the two products are *technically complementary;* (b) when an increase in one product causes the marginal coefficient of production of the other product to increase, that is, when the derivative $\frac{\partial^2 v}{\partial x\, \partial y}$ is positive, we shall say that the products are *technically competing;* and (c) when an increase in one product does not influence the marginal coefficient of production of the other product, that is, when the derivative $\frac{\partial^2 v}{\partial x\, \partial y}$ is zero, we shall say that the products are *technically independent*. We thus have the following classification of joint production with reference to the nature of the mixed derivative of v:

$$\frac{\partial^2 v}{\partial x\, \partial y} < 0 \ \ldots \ \text{technically complementary products}$$

$$\frac{\partial^2 v}{\partial x\, \partial y} > 0 \ \ldots \ \text{technically competing products}$$

$$\frac{\partial^2 v}{\partial x\, \partial y} = 0 \ \ldots \ \text{technically independent products.}[1]$$

---

[1] Since we have written the production functions in the form
$$x = \varphi_{(x)}\, (v,\ y)$$
and
$$y = \varphi_{(y)}\, (v,\ x)$$
the technical interrelation between the products can be expressed only in relation to the marginal coefficients of production, and not to the

If we now observe certain products such as gas and coke, or cotton and cotton seed, which are commonly referred to as products of joint production, it will be seen that they generally belong to the class here defined as technically complementary products, and that they are probably technically complementary for all ranges of output.[1] More commonly, however, we shall find that two products, jointly produced, which may be classified as technically complementary at certain outputs may, on the other hand, be technically independent or even technically competing at other outputs. When, for example, rails and construction steel are jointly produced by the same plant, these products may be technically complementary as long as the plant is working at a low capacity, while they become technically independent or technically competing as soon as higher

---

marginal productivities. The marginal productivity of v with respect to x is defined at a constant value of y. In order to express the relationship between a change in y and the marginal productivity with respect to x, we should need the derivative $\frac{\partial^2 x}{\partial y \partial v}$. But this derivative does not exist, since the variable v necessarily must change for an increase of y, when x is constant.

We may notice the similarity between our production theory and the general theory of utility. In the classical formulation of the utility theory two products, x and y, are classified as complementary, competing or independent, as the derivative $\frac{\partial^2 \varphi}{\partial x \partial y}$ of their total utility, φ, is positive, negative or zero. [Cf. e. g. Pareto, *Manuel, op. cit.* pp. 252 ff, Edgeworth, "The Pure Theory of Monopoly", *Papers Relating to Political Economy*, vol. I (London, 1925) pp. 116—17 and Amoroso, *Lezioni, op. cit.* pp. 92 ff.] The three relationships in our technical classification are the reverse of these because the input of v corresponds to the "disutility" instead of to the utility of the products.

The classical concepts of complementary, competing and independent products, which assume that the utility of different products can be measured in absolute terms, have, however, lately been re-examined and revised on the ground that such a measurement cannot be made. [Cf. J. R. Hicks and R. G. D. Allen, "A Reconsideration of the Theory of Value", *Economica*, New Series, I (1934) pp. 52—76 and 196—219.] An analogous revision of the concepts of complementary, competing and independent products in the theory of production might be made, but is not necessary since in the production theory we deal with physically measurable quantities.

[1] For examples of complementary ("joint") and competing ("rival") products in the chemical industry, see T. J. Kreps, "Joint Cost in the Chemical Industry", *Q. J. E.* XLIV (1929/30) p. 458: "Thus, for example, in the electrolytic soda and chlorine industry, caustic soda and chlorine are joint products. But liquid chlorine and bleaching solution are rival products."

outputs are reached. In other words, though it is possible under certain conditions to classify two products as technically complementary in a general sense, there are other conditions under which the technical interdependence of the products may vary in nature from time to time or from one plant to another.

2. *The relationship between costs and output.* — In how far, then, does this technical interdependence between the products influence the relationship between costs and output? In thinking of the firm's cost we shall, as before, distinguish between the fixed cost, C_F, which is constant, and the variable cost, C_V, which varies when the output varies. The sum of the fixed cost and the variable cost is the total cost, C_T; and the total cost of the joint output of the two products is less than the sum of the total costs would be if the two products were produced separately. There would be no inducement for joint production were this not true.

We are by assumption dealing with a production which uses only one single variable service. The cost of this service represents the variable cost of output. If, as before, we denote the amount of the service used by v, and denote its price by q, we may write the variable cost as equal to q times v. Since this q is either a constant or a function of v, and since v, in its turn, is a function of the quantities of the products x and y [equation (1 c)], the variable cost, and the total cost, which is the sum of the variable cost and the fixed cost, also become functions of x and y. Thus we may write

$$C_T = C(x, y) = qv + C_F.$$

At this point we may notice an important difference between the present case and the case of simple production. When only one product was produced, we could divide the variable and total costs by the quantity of output and obtain the average variable and the average total costs. In the present case, where we have two products of entirely different kind and the variable and total costs of product x are inseparable from the costs of product y, such average costs do not exist. Only at the production margin can we speak of separate costs for the two products — their marginal costs.[1] These marginal costs we obtain as before by a differentiation of the cost function. Thus, if we assume the price of the productive service to be constant, we have the marginal cost of x and y

$$C_{M_x} = \frac{\partial C_T}{\partial x} = q\,\frac{\partial v}{\partial x} \quad \text{and} \quad C_{M_y} = \frac{\partial C_T}{\partial y} = q\,\frac{\partial v}{\partial y}.$$

The behaviour of the marginal costs is determined by the second partial derivatives $\dfrac{\partial^2 C_T}{\partial x^2}$ and $\dfrac{\partial^2 C_T}{\partial y^2}$, and by the mixed derivative $\dfrac{\partial^2 C_T}{\partial x\,\partial y}$. When the service price is a constant the first two of these derivatives become

$$\frac{\partial^2 C_T}{\partial x^2} = q\,\frac{\partial^2 v}{\partial x^2} \quad \text{and} \quad \frac{\partial^2 C_T}{\partial y^2} = q\,\frac{\partial^2 v}{\partial y^2}$$

which are both assumed to be positive after a certain minimum output has been reached. The mixed derivative

$$\frac{\partial^2 C_T}{\partial x\,\partial y} = q\,\frac{\partial^2 v}{\partial x\,\partial y}$$

may be either negative, zero, or positive, depending on the nature of the derivative $\dfrac{\partial^2 v}{\partial x\,\partial y}$. But this last derivative $\dfrac{\partial^2 v}{\partial x\,\partial y}$ constituted the basis for our classification of joint production. We therefore have the following relations with reference to this classification:

$$\frac{\partial^2 C_T}{\partial x\,\partial y} < 0 \;\ldots\ldots\; \text{technically complementary products,}$$

---

[1] If this fundamental characteristic of joint production were perfectly clear to all contributors to cost accounting literature, most of the futile discussion about how general costs shall be allocated to different products would vanish, and one would instead concentrate on the really important problem of the behaviour of the marginal costs.

$$\frac{\partial^2 C_T}{\partial x \, \partial y} > 0 \ \ldots \ldots \text{ technically competing products, and}$$

$$\frac{\partial^2 C_I}{\partial x \, \partial y} = 0 \ \ldots \ldots \text{ technically independent products.}$$

In other words, an increase in the output of one of the products will decrease, increase or leave unchanged the marginal cost of the other product, when the two products are respectively technically complementary, competing, or independent. The reverse relationship also holds true: that is, when an increase in the output of one of the products decreases, increases, or leaves unchanged the marginal cost of the other product, it follows that the two products must be respectively technically complementary, competing, or independent.

We must notice, however, that the general validity of these relations depends on the assumption of a constant service price. Should the price of the variable service vary with the quantity of the service used, we may have a situation where the effect of the technical interdependence of the products on the costs is offset by the change of the service price. If, for example, the service price increases with the quantity of the service, it may very well happen that $\frac{\partial^2 C_T}{\partial x \, \partial y}$ becomes positive although the two products are technically complementary; or, conversely, that the two products are technically complementary in spite of the fact that the derivative $\frac{\partial^2 C_T}{\partial x \, \partial y}$ is positive.[1] We must therefore distinguish between the effects on the costs of a variation in the prices of a productive service and in the technical interdependence between the products; only the latter effect is of interest at the present.

---

[1] If q is a function of v, we have

$$\frac{\partial^2 C_T}{\partial x \partial y} = \frac{\partial^2 v}{\partial x \partial y} \left(q + v \frac{dq}{dv} \right) + 2 \frac{\partial v}{\partial x} \frac{\partial v}{\partial y} \frac{dq}{qv} + v \frac{\partial v}{\partial x} \frac{\partial v}{\partial y} \frac{\partial^2 q}{dv^2}$$

an expression which may be positive, zero, or negative when the derivative $\frac{\partial^2 v}{\partial x \partial y}$ is negative, but the derivative $\frac{dq}{dv}$ is positive.

Outline of a General Theory of Joint Production.

Before we proceed to a discussion of the demand conditions or the maximization problems of joint production, let us try to extend our analysis to a more general case. We shall still assume that our firm produces only two products, but we shall abandon the assumption of a single variable productive service. Our task is to show how such a change in our assumptions influences the relationships and classifications of joint production already established.

1. *The relationship between input and output.* — If we start with the technical problem of production, we notice that the output of the two products will now depend upon the inputs of a series of variable services rather than upon one alone. If these different inputs are denoted by $v_1, \ldots, v_n$, we have the production functions of x and y

(2 a) $$x = \varphi_{(x)} (v_1, \ldots, v_n, y)$$

and

(2 b) $$y = \varphi_{(y)} (v_1, \ldots, v_n, x).$$

These functions are of the same general character as in the previous case. Hence, if they are differentiated partially with respect to the different services, we get the marginal productivities for the two products; while, if the former function $\varphi_{(x)}$ is differentiated partially with respect to y, or if the latter function $\varphi_{(y)}$ is differentiated partially with respect to x, we get the technical substitution relation between the products at a given input of the productive services. These different derivatives, we may assume, have the same properties as in the case discussed above; that is

$$\frac{\partial x}{\partial v_1}, \ldots, \frac{\partial x}{\partial v_n} > 0, \quad \frac{\partial y}{\partial v_1}, \ldots, \frac{\partial y}{\partial v_n} > 0$$

and, when the service quantities are the same in the two functions,

$$\frac{\partial x}{\partial y} = \frac{1}{\dfrac{\partial y}{\partial x}} < 0.$$

The total differential of x, when y is constant (and therefore treated as a parameter), and the total differential of y when x is constant, we write

(3 a) $\qquad dx = \dfrac{\partial x}{\partial v_1} dv_1 + \ldots + \dfrac{\partial x}{\partial v_n} dv_n \qquad (y = \text{constant})$

and

(3 b) $\qquad dy = \dfrac{\partial y}{\partial v_1} dv_1 + \ldots + \dfrac{\partial y}{\partial v_n} dv_r \qquad (x = \text{constant}).$

From this it follows that when the output of one of the products is constant, the increment produced in the other product by an infinitesimal change of the variable services is equal to the sum of the marginal products of the services. A similar relation was observed earlier in the case of simple production.[1]

It is when we arrive at the problem of classification that the present, general case first becomes fundamentally different from the elementary case earlier considered. In the earlier case we could express the input of the single variable service as a function of the two products x and y exclusively. This function gave us the two marginal coefficients of production and the mixed derivative $\dfrac{\partial^2 v}{\partial x \, \partial y}$.

---

[1] It should be noticed that if we fix the proportion of the two products in a certain ratio $x/y = a$, the quantity, z, of such a fixed product combination produced, may be written

$$z = \varphi \, (v_1, \ldots, v_n).$$

With respect to this z we therefore have the same technical relations as with respect to a single output, namely

$$dz = \frac{\partial z}{\partial v_1} dv_1 + \ldots + \frac{\partial z}{\partial v_n} dv_n$$

and

$$\varepsilon \cdot z = \frac{\partial z}{\partial v_1} v_1 + \ldots + \frac{\partial z}{\partial v_n} v_n$$

where ε is the function coefficient defined as before (compare p. 17 above). But we must notice that the function coefficient here refers to a given ratio a of the two products, and that it varies when a varies. Where formerly we could illustrate the variations of the function coefficient on a two-dimensional diagram in a two-service case, we should now need three dimensions for the same purpose (the third axis representing the ratio a of the two products).

It was with reference to the properties of this derivative that we made our classification of joint production. In the present case, on the other hand, we have a series of different services which can be substituted for one another. The input of one service will, therefore, depend no longer only upon the quantities of the two products, but will depend also upon the quantities of the other services. Using the same symbols as before, we may write the input of the service v_k as a function

$$(2\ c)\quad v_k = \psi_k\,(x,\ y,\ v_1,\ \ldots,\ v_{k-1},\ v_{k+1},\ \ldots,\ v_n)$$

and we shall have n such functions, one for every service. But since we have n productive services, we must also have n different coefficients of production for every product, and n mixed derivatives $\dfrac{\partial^2 v}{\partial x\ \partial y}$ instead of one as in the previous case. If we still want to base our production classification on the properties of the derivatives $\dfrac{\partial^2 v}{\partial x\ \partial y}$, we can do so only on one of two assumtions: *either* that the properties of the derivatives are all of the same kind, that is, that the output of one of the products always influences the different coefficients of production of the other service in the same way, which probably seldom happens; *or* that the properties of the derivatives can be compared with one another and averaged, that is, that we can compare and weigh the influence of an output change on the different coefficients of production. Such a comparison or weighing requires, however, that the different services are expressed in the same unit, and the only unit common to all the services is their cost. In order to find a measure of the technical interdependence of the products when several variable services are employed, and to obtain a general criterion for our classification of joint production we must, therefore, go to the relationship between costs and output.

2. *The expansion paths of joint production.* — Proceeding to the cost problems of production, we meet another differ-

ence between the present general case of joint production and the elementary case considered above. When several variable services are employed in a production there exist a number of possible service combinations and of possible costs for every output. We must therefore first find the combinations of lowest cost for the different outputs, or, to express the same thing in a more familiar way, find the *expansion paths* for the two products. This problem did not, of course, exist when only one variable service was employed. As in the case of simple production, the lowest cost combinations may be arrived at through a process of gradual substitution between the different services. At the substitution margin a service v_k has a *marginal unit cost*

$$c_k = q_k \left(1 + \lambda_k \right)$$

where q_k is the price and λ_k is the price flexibility of the service, and a marginal productivity with respect to each one of the products

$$\frac{\partial x}{\partial v_k} \quad \text{and} \quad \frac{\partial y}{\partial v_k}.$$

The relationship between the marginal unit cost and the marginal productivity we again define as the *cost-productivity ratio of the service*, but in this case we have two cost-productivity ratios for every service

$$_xc_k = \frac{q_k \left(1 + \lambda_k \right)}{\dfrac{\partial x}{\partial v_k}} \quad \text{and} \quad _yc_k = \frac{q_k \left(1 + \lambda_k \right)}{\dfrac{\partial y}{\partial v_k}}.$$

On analogy to the case of simple production, the minimum cost of a given output is reached when the marginal unit costs of the different services are proportional to the marginal productivities of the services with respect to each one of the products, i. e. when the cost-productivity ratios of the differ-services with respect to each one of the products are equal.

$$(4) \quad \begin{cases} q_1(1 + \lambda_1) : \ldots \ldots : q_n(1 + \lambda_n) = \\ \quad = \dfrac{\partial x}{\partial v_1} : \ldots \ldots : \dfrac{\partial x}{\partial v_n} \\ \quad = \dfrac{\partial y}{\partial v_1} : \ldots \ldots : \dfrac{\partial y}{\partial v_n} \end{cases}$$

or

$$_xc_1 = {}_xc_2 = \ldots \ldots = {}_xc_n \text{ and } {}_yc_1 = {}_yc_2 = \ldots \ldots = {}_yc_n.$$

Should the marginal productivity of a service with respect to any one of the products be larger in relation to its marginal unit cost than the marginal productivities of the other services in relation to their marginal unit costs, it would obviously be profitable to substitute this service for the other services, and *vice versa*. The expansion paths of a joint output are thus determined by exactly the same relations as determine the expansion path of a single product. The difference is that with a joint output there are, for every service, two cost-productivity ratios whose relative magnitudes are still to be determined.

3. *The relationships between costs and output.* — With the expansion paths as given, the relationship between costs and output becomes in the main the same as in the case of a single variable service. The variable cost will depend on the inputs of the variable services along the expansion path, which in their turn will depend on the quantities of the two products produced. Again, we may write the variable cost and the total cost, which is the sum of the variable cost and the fixed cost (C_F), as functions of x and y. Using the same symbols as before we have

$$C_T = C(x, y) = \Sigma q_k v_k + C_F$$
$$k = 1, \ldots, n.[1]$$

---

[1] It should be noticed that if we fix the proportions between the two products in a given ratio $x/y = a$ which is produced in the quantity z, the relationship between the costs and the output z becomes exactly the same as the relationship between the costs and a single product as discussed in chapter III. Thus, when the service prices are constant and the expansion path is a straight line starting from the point of origin we may, for example, write the average variable cost of z equal to the function coefficient times the marginal cost of z

$$C_{AV} = \varepsilon \cdot \frac{dC}{dz}$$

where the function coefficient relates to the chosen ratio a of the two products. Cf. above p. 85 note 1.

If we differentiate the variable cost with respect to x and y, we obtain the marginal costs of the two products, and, as in the case of simple production, we find that these marginal costs are on the expansion path equal to the cost-productivity ratios of the productive services with respect to x and y.

$$\frac{\partial C}{\partial x} = {}_xc_1 = {}_xc_2 = \ldots = {}_xc_n$$

(5) and

$$\frac{\partial C}{\partial y} = {}_yc_1 = {}_yc_2 = \ldots = {}_yc_n{}^1.$$

As in the elementary case earlier discussed the marginal cost of product x, for example, may be assumed to vary with the quantity of the product produced, and generally in such a way that when the other product y is constant and x increases, the marginal cost of x first decreases or remains constant and later increases. That is, we may

---

[1] The marginal cost of the product x expresses the relationship between infinitesimal increments of the costs and of the product, when the other product y remains constant. If the costs are given by the function

$$C = f(v_1, \ldots, v_n)$$

and the quantity of x by the function

$$x = \varphi_{(x)}(v_1, \ldots, v_n, y)$$

where y is to be regarded as a parameter, we get the increment of the costs

$$dC = \frac{\partial C}{\partial v_1} dv_1 + \ldots + \frac{\partial C}{\partial v_n} \partial v_n$$

and the increment of the product

$$dx = \frac{\partial x}{\partial v_1} dv_1 + \ldots + \frac{\partial x}{\partial v_n} dv_n.$$

But $\frac{\partial C}{\partial v_1} = q_1(1 + \lambda_1)$, $\frac{\partial C}{\partial v_2} = q_2(1 + \lambda_2)$ etc., and on the expansion path we have

$$q_1(1 + \lambda_1) = {}_xc_1 \frac{\partial x}{\partial v_1}, \quad q_2(1 + \lambda_2) = {}_xc_2 \frac{\partial x}{\partial v_2} \text{ etc.}$$

where ${}_xc_1 = {}_xc_2 = \ldots = {}_xc_n$. Substituting these relationships in the two differentials above, we get

$$\frac{dC}{dx} = {}_xc_1 = {}_xc_2 = \ldots {}_xc_n.$$

A similar proof may be given for the marginal cost of y.

assume the second cost derivative $\dfrac{\partial^2 C}{\partial x^2}$ first to be negative or zero and later to be positive. The same relations hold true for the other product.[1]

But the marginal cost of x may also vary with a change in the other product y, that is, the mixed derivative $\dfrac{\partial^2 C}{\partial x\,\partial y}$ may be either greater or less than zero, and for either of two reasons: (1) because the prices of the services change with the inputs; or (2) because the products are technically interdependent. The first of these possibilities may be of great practical importance — it is often the expected economies of large-scale buying that represent the main inducement to joint production — but this is not a problem that is relevant at the moment. Let us instead consider the question of technical interdependence. In the elementary case given above we observed that when two products were technically complementary, competing or independent, an increment of one of the products respectively decreased, increased or left unchanged the marginal cost of the other. When the service prices were constant, these relationships could also be reversed; that is, from the fact that the marginal cost of one of the products decreased, increased or remained constant with an increase of the other product, it followed that the two products were respectively technically complementary, competing or independent. In the present general case where several variable services are employed, and where it is impossible to measure the technical interdependence of the products in purely technical terms, we must start out from the relationships between cost and output. On

---

[1] An interesting attempt to determine statistically the cost function and the marginal costs of two joint products, freight service and passenger service, of certain American railroads is made by W. L. Crum [Cf. "The Statistical Allocation of Joint Costs", *Journal of The American Statistical Association*, XXI (1926), pp. 9—24.] With reference to the results of a multiple correlation between the expenses per mile as the dependent variable and the ton-miles per mile and passenger-miles per mile as the independent variables, Crum concludes "that an increase of one ton-mile in freight traffic density increases the expenses per mile by .33 cents, and an increase of one passenger-mile in passenger traffic density increases the expenses by 1.8 cents ...".

analogy to the "reversed" relationships of the previous case we therefore define two products as technically complementary, competing, or independent when, the service prices being constant, the marginal cost of one of the products decreases, increases or remains unchanged with an increase of the product, that is, as the mixed derivative $\frac{\partial^2 C}{\partial x \, \partial y}$ is negative, positive or zero.[1] But the actual properties of this derivative, which may be different for different plants or for different levels of output at the same plant, can, of course, only be known from practical experience in the particular case.

4. *The demand conditions of joint production.* — In the present chapter we have been trying to examine the particular features of the different production determining forces which apply to the case of joint production but which did not appear when the firm produced only one single commodity. Thus far our study has been concerned solely with the technical aspects and the cost aspects of production. Still to be examined are the supply conditions of capital funds and the demand conditions for the firm's output. With regard to the first of these conditions: the supply of capital, we notice immediately that it must be the same irrespective of whether a single product or a joint output is produced. The amount of privately owned funds which exists at the beginning of the period, or the conditions under which the firm can borrow outside funds, are independent of whether the firm employs its capital in a simple or in a joint production. What was said earlier with regard to the capital supply must, therefore, be assumed to hold also in the present case.

---

[1] For a similar classification of joint production, where, however, the condition of constant service prices is not definitely stated, compare Edgeworth, "The Pure Theory of Monopoly", *Papers, op. cit.*, vol. 1, p. 127: "In symbols let x and y be the respective quantities produced and $\varphi(x, y)$ the expenses, or, more generally, the pecuniary measure of the real cost of the productions of x and y together; we have then case (a) if $\frac{d^2\varphi}{dx, dy}$ is positive; if it is negative, case (b).

These relations may be designed by the terms (a) rival production, (b) complementary production." See also his "Laws of Increasing and Diminishing Returns", *Papers, op. cit.*, vol. 1, pp. 86—87.

The same similarity between simple and joint production cannot be observed when we pass to the conditions of demand. In the case of simple production we have a single product and a single anticipated price which we have assumed is determined exclusively by the quantity of the product sold. In joint production we have two different products, each with its own anticipated price; but more than that, the separate demands for the two products may be so interrelated that the price of one product depends not only, as before, upon the quantity in which it is produced, but also upon the quantity of the other product. Because of this possible interrelation between two distinct demands, we must now write the product prices, p_x and p_y, as functions of two variables, x and y, instead of one, at least in the general case.

$$p_x = p_x (x, y)$$
$$p_y = p_y (x, y).$$

These are the demand functions of joint production. We shall assume, for the properties of these functions, that the price of a product always varies inversely with its quantity; that is, we shall assume the price derivatives $\frac{\partial p_x}{\partial x}$ and $\frac{\partial p_y}{\partial y}$ always to be negative. The effect of a change in the quantity of one product upon the price of the other product, on the other hand, may vary from case to case: the derivatives $\frac{\partial p_x}{\partial y}$ and $\frac{\partial p_y}{\partial x}$ may be either positive or negative. Irrespective of whether these derivatives are positive or negative, however, they may always be expected to be of the same sign, because if an increase in the commodity x has an increasing or decreasing effect on the price of y, it seems quite certain that an increase in the commodity y will also have an increasing or decreasing effect on the price of x. As examples of products from the same plant which have increasing effects on each other's prices we may mention gasoline and lubricating oil for automobile consumption. Examples of products which instead have decreasing effects on each other's prices may be found in different varieties of the same "commodity" such as black and brown shoes, or roadster and sedan automobiles.

If we write the product prices as functions of the outputs x and y we may also write the total revenue, which is equal to the sum of the two outputs multiplied by their respective prices, as a function of x and y.

$$E_T = p_x x + p_y y = E_T(x, y).$$

From this function we get the marginal revenues

$$E_{M_x} = \frac{\partial E_T}{\partial x} = p_x + x \frac{\partial p_x}{\partial x} + y \frac{\partial p_y}{\partial x}$$

and

$$E_{M_y} = \frac{\partial E_T}{\partial y} = x \frac{\partial p_x}{\partial y} + p_y + y \frac{\partial p_y}{\partial y}.$$

Thus it follows that the marginal revenue from one of the products is generally determined not only by the increase in revenue from that product itself, as when only one product is sold, but also by the change in the revenue from the other product. This latter change may be positive or negative as the products have increasing or decreasing effects on each other's prices. It is only when the demands for the two products are independent of each other, that is, when the derivatives $\frac{\partial p_x}{\partial y}$ and $\frac{\partial p_y}{\partial x}$ are zero, that the marginal revenue of one product is determined exclusively by its own sale, and we are able to write

$$E_{M_x} = p_x \left(\mathbf{1} + \lambda_{p_x}\right) \quad \text{and} \quad E_{M_y} = p_y \left(\mathbf{1} + \lambda_{p_y}\right)$$

where the λ's, as before, denote the simple price flexibilities of the products.

The relationship between the marginal revenues and the outputs is most clearly characterized by the properties of the second derivatives $\frac{\partial^2 E_T}{\partial x^2}$, $\frac{\partial^2 E_T}{\partial y^2}$ and $\frac{\partial^2 E_T}{\partial x \partial y}$. The first two of these derivatives, we may assume, are generally negative. If the output of one of the products increases while the output of the other product remains constant, the total revenue will increase, but probably only at a decreasing rate. The derivative $\frac{\partial^2 E}{\partial x\,\partial y}$, on the other hand, which we may write

$$\frac{\partial^2 E}{\partial x\,\partial y} = \frac{\partial p_x}{\partial y} + x\,\frac{\partial^2 p_x}{\partial x\,\partial y} + y\,\frac{\partial^2 p_y}{\partial x\,\partial y} + \frac{\partial p_y}{\partial x}$$

may be positive, negative or zero, depending on the signs of these different price derivatives. When for a large range of output the two products consistently have increasing or decreasing effects on each other's prices — that is, when for a large range of output the price derivatives $\frac{\partial p_x}{\partial y}$ and $\frac{\partial p_y}{\partial x}$ are consistently positive or negative — it seems likely that the derivative $\frac{\partial^2 E}{\partial x\,\partial y}$ will also be positive or negative. For in this case we may assume either that the mixed price derivatives $\frac{\partial^2 p_x}{\partial x\,\partial y}$ and $\frac{\partial^2 p_y}{\partial y\,\partial x}$ are of the same sign as the derivatives $\frac{\partial p_x}{\partial y}$ and $\frac{\partial p_y}{\partial x}$, or, when they are of opposite sign, that their effect is negligible, since the derivatives $\frac{\partial^3 p_x}{\partial^2 x\,\partial y}$ and $\frac{\partial^3 p_y}{\partial^2 y\,\partial x}$ probably have the same sign as the first derivatives. When, however, the two products have an increasing or decreasing effect on each other's prices within a narrow range of output only, it may be possible that the derivatives $\frac{\partial^3 p_x}{\partial^2 x\,\partial y}$ and $\frac{\partial^3 p_y}{\partial^2 y\,\partial x}$ are of opposite sign to the first derivatives and that the same will consequently be the case with the derivative $\frac{\partial^2 E}{\partial x\,\partial y}$. The final determination of these different price relations, which are often of great relevance to the firm's price and sales policy — for example, in the selection of suitable "loss leaders" — can, however, not be made on *a priori* ground but only from actual experience. Here we shall only refer to the derivative $\dfrac{\partial^2 E}{\partial x\,\partial y}$, and we shall classify two products as *complementary*, *competing* or *independent in demand*, as this derivative is positive, negative or zero, that is, as an increase in the sale of one of the products increases, decreases or leaves unchanged the marginal revenue of the other product. The complementarity of demand of two or several products represents another inducement for the firm to enter into joint production of several commodities.

THE RATE OF RETURN AND THE MAXIMUM CONDITIONS.

After this review of the different production determining forces and their influence on the costs and revenues of a joint output, we are ready to attack the maximization problem. We are faced with a firm which in a certain period produces two joint products. At the beginning of the period the firm starts out with a given amount of capital, which, together with borrowed funds, it invests in the production of the two products. The purpose of the investment is to maximize the rate of return on the firm's capital.

1. *The rate of return and the marginal rate of return.* — As in the case of simple production, we see the net return of the firm's activity as the difference between the total revenue and the total cost, inclusive of interest cost. If, as before, we write the interest cost iL, where i is the interest rate and L the amount borrowed, we get the net return

$$(6) \qquad R = E_T - (C_T + iL)$$

The rate of return, r, is obtained if we express the net return as a rate on the firm's capital, K, during the period

$$(7) \qquad r = \frac{R}{K} = \frac{E_T - (C_T + iL)}{K}.$$

So far, the maximization problem of joint production is no different from the maximization problem of simple production. The first difference comes when we introduce the concepts of marginal return and marginal rate of return. The marginal return we have earlier defined as the difference between the marginal revenue of a product and its marginal cost *exclusive* of interest cost; the marginal rate of return is merely the marginal return expressed as a rate on the marginal increment of investment, which is equal to the marginal cost of the product. We now have two products, each one with its marginal revenue and marginal cost. Consequently we have also two marginal returns, one for each product,

$$R_{M_x} = E_{M_x} - C_{M_x}$$

(8) and

$$R_{M_y} = E_{M_y} - C_{M_y}$$

and two marginal rates of return

$$r_{M_x} = \frac{E_{M_x} - C_{M_x}}{C_{M_x}}$$

(9) and

$$r_{M_y} = \frac{E_{M_y} - C_{M_y}}{C_{M_y}}.$$

2. *The maximum conditions.* — We have earlier observed that the total revenue and the total cost of a joint output are exclusively determined by the separate quantities of the two products produced, and that they can both be written as functions of x and y. From this it follows that the rate of return, which depends on the difference between the total revenue and the total cost, is also determined exclusively by the quantities of the products, and may be written as a function

$$r = r(x, y).$$

Our task is to determine the maximum of this function. From the calculus we know[1] that a function of two variables

---

[1] See e. g. F. S. Woods, *Advanced Calculus, op. cit.* p. 117.

has a maximum when

$$\frac{\partial r}{\partial x} = 0 \quad \text{and} \quad \frac{\partial r}{\partial y} = 0,$$

the necessary conditions, and when

$$\frac{\partial^2 r}{\partial x^2} < 0 \quad \text{and} \quad \frac{\partial^2 r}{\partial y^2} < 0,$$

the sufficient conditions. There is also another necessary condition

$$\left[\frac{\partial^2 r}{\partial x \, \partial y}\right]^2 < \frac{\partial^2 r}{\partial x^2} \frac{\partial^2 r}{\partial y^2},$$

but in the case of cost and revenue functions this condition can always be assumed to hold true.

Let us start with the partial derivative of r with respect to the product x, which we write

$$\frac{\partial r}{\partial x} = \frac{\partial E_T}{\partial x} - \frac{\partial C_T}{\partial x} - \frac{d(iL)}{dL} \frac{\partial L}{\partial x}.$$

But $\dfrac{d(iL)}{dL}$ is equal to the marginal rate of interest, i_M,[1] and $\dfrac{\partial L}{\partial x}$ to the marginal cost $\dfrac{\partial C}{\partial x}$. We therefore get

$$\frac{\partial r}{\partial x} = \frac{\partial E_T}{\partial x} - \frac{\partial C_T}{\partial x}(1 + i_M) = 0$$

and similarly the partial derivative of r with respect to y

$$\frac{\partial r}{\partial y} = \frac{\partial E_T}{\partial y} - \frac{\partial C_T}{\partial y}(1 + i_M) = 0$$

If we introduce the notations E_M and C_M for the marginal revenues and the marginal costs, we get

$$E_{M_x} = C_{M_x}(1 + i_M)$$

---

[1] Cf. chapter IV, p. 60.

98

(10) and

$$E_{M_y} = C_{M_y} \ (1 + i_M),$$

or when we write the same relationships in another way

$$\frac{E_{M_x} - C_{M_x}}{C_{M_x}} = r_{M_x} = i_M$$

and

$$\frac{E_{M_y} - C_{M_y}}{C_{M_y}} = r_{M_y} = i_M$$

which give us the equality

(10 a) $$r_{M_x} = r_{M_y} = i_M.$$

On perfect analogy with the case of simple production we thus see that in order to receive a maximum rate of return on its capital, the firm will expand its production of each one of the joint products till their marginal revenues become equal to their marginal cost, inclusive of interest cost,[1] or, which is the same thing, till for both products the marginal rate of return becomes equal to the marginal rate of interest.[2] We may notice, however, that the mar-

---

[1] Cf. Marshall, *Principles, op. cit.*, p. 854: "If in equilibrium x' oxen annually are supplied and sold at a price $y' = \Phi(x')$; and each ox yields m units of beef: and if breeders find that by modifying the breeding and feeding of oxen they can increase their meat-yielding properties to the extent of Δm units of beef (the hides and other joint products being, on the balance, unaltered), and that the extra expense of doing this is $\Delta y'$, then $\frac{\Delta y'}{\Delta m}$ represents the marginal supply price of beef: if this price were less than the selling price, it would be to the interest of the breeders to make the change."

[2] The nature of this maximum condition may be made clear by a graphical illustration. In the adjoining diagram, whose axes represent

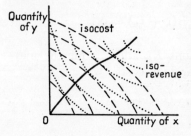

the quantities, x and y, of the two products, and in which, therefore, different points signify different product combinations, we combine (a) by one set of curves, the *isorevenues*, all product combinations which yield the same revenue; and (b) by another set of curves, the *product isocosts*, all product combinations which have the same costs, inclusive of interest costs. The two sets of curves intersect each other in an infinite number

ginal revenue of a product includes here not only the revenue increase of the product itself but also the change in the revenue of the other product.

The sufficient conditions for a maximum rate of return we obtain by a second differentiation of equation (7):

$$\frac{\partial^2 r}{\partial x^2} = \frac{\partial^2 E}{\partial x^2} - \frac{\partial}{\partial x}\left[\frac{\partial C}{\partial x}(1 + i_M)\right] < 0$$

of points. (Cf. Stackelberg, *Kostentheorie, op. cit.*, pp. 62 ff.) The isorevenues are defined by the equation

$$E(x, y) = \text{constant}$$

and the product isocosts by the equation

$$C(x, y) = \text{constant}.$$

The tangents of the two sets of curves may consequently be written for the isorevenues

$$\left[\frac{dy}{dx}\right]_{(E)} = -\frac{\dfrac{\partial E}{\partial x}}{\dfrac{\partial E}{\partial y}}$$

and for the product isocosts

$$\left[\frac{dy}{dx}\right]_{(C)} = -\frac{\dfrac{\partial C}{\partial x}(1 + i_M)}{\dfrac{\partial C}{\partial y}(1 + i_M)}.$$

In the case of perfect competition when the prices of the products are constant, the isorevenues become straight lines with a negative slope equal to the relationship between the given prices.

In order to maximize the rate of return, the firm will substitute the two products along an isorevenue till the lowest cost is reached, a substitution analogous to the substitution which the firm makes between the productive services in order to reach the expansion path of production. In fact, we may speak even here of an expansion path. The location of this path will depend on the relative variation of the two sets of curves. If the isorevenues are more concave to the axes than the isocosts, a given isorevenue will pass lower and lower isocosts the nearer we come to the axes, and the minimum cost for a given revenue combination will be obtained when only one product is produced. If, on the other hand, the isorevenues are less concave than the isocosts, as in the figure, a given isorevenue will intersect higher isocosts near the axes than in the middle of the diagram. The minimum cost combinations are then obtained on a path where the isorevenues are tangent to the "lowest possible" isocosts, that is, where

$$\frac{\dfrac{\partial E}{\partial x}}{\dfrac{\partial E}{\partial y}} = \frac{\dfrac{\partial C}{\partial x}(1 + i_M)}{\dfrac{\partial C}{\partial y}(1 + i_M)}$$

and the most profitable point on the path is reached when the marginal revenues of the two products become equal to their respective marginal costs, inclusive of interest cost.

and

$$\frac{\partial^2 r}{\partial y^2} = \frac{\partial^2 E}{\partial y^2} - \frac{\partial}{\partial y}\left[\frac{\partial C}{\partial y}\left(1 + i_M\right)\right] < 0.$$

As in the case of simple production, these conditions are fulfilled when the marginal costs of the products, inclusive of interest costs, increase more rapidly than the marginal revenues.

In addition to these different conditions it is given, as before, that the maximum rate of return, thus determined, must exceed or at least be equal to the rate of interest which the firm would obtain if it invested its funds outside the present activity.

3. *The maximum conditions and the production determining forces.* — Before we end our discussion of joint production, let us try to coordinate the results thus far obtained. We have observed that the minimum cost of a certain product combination is reached when the cost-productivity ratios of the productive services with respect to the two products are equal between themselves and equal to the marginal costs [equations (4) and (5)]. These equalities hold true whether interest costs are considered or not. We have further observed that when the rate of return is maximum, the marginal revenue of each one of the products is equal to the corresponding marginal cost, inclusive of interest cost [equation (10)]. From these relationships it follows that for a maximum rate of return the respective marginal revenues must be equal to the cost-productivity ratios of the productive services with respect to the two products, inclusive of interest costs. That is,

$$\frac{\partial E_T}{\partial x} = \frac{q_1\left(1 + \lambda_1\right)}{\dfrac{\partial x}{\partial v_1}}\left(1 + i_M\right) = \ldots = \frac{q_n\left(1 + \lambda_n\right)}{\dfrac{\partial x}{\partial v_n}}\left(1 + i_M\right)$$

and

$$\frac{\partial E_T}{\partial y} = \frac{q_1\left(1 + \lambda_1\right)}{\dfrac{\partial y}{\partial v_1}}\left(1 + i_M\right) = \ldots = \frac{q_n\left(1 + \lambda_n\right)}{\dfrac{\partial y}{\partial v_n}}\left(1 + i_M\right)$$

or, if the equations are written in another form

$$q_1\left(\mathbf{I}+\lambda_1\right)=\frac{\mathbf{I}}{\mathbf{I}+i_M}\frac{\partial E_T}{\partial x}\frac{\partial x}{\partial v_1}=\frac{\mathbf{I}}{\mathbf{I}+i_M}\frac{\partial E_T}{\partial y}\frac{\partial y}{\partial v_1}$$

$$q_2\left(\mathbf{I}+\lambda_2\right)=\frac{\mathbf{I}}{\mathbf{I}+i_M}\frac{\partial E_T}{\partial x}\frac{\partial x}{\partial v_2}=\frac{\mathbf{I}}{\mathbf{I}+i_M}\frac{\partial E_T}{\partial y}\frac{\partial y}{\partial v_2}$$

. . . .
. . . .

$$q_n\left(\mathbf{I}+\lambda_n\right)=\frac{\mathbf{I}}{\mathbf{I}+i_M}\frac{\partial E_T}{\partial x}\cdot\frac{\partial x}{\partial v_n}=\frac{\mathbf{I}}{\mathbf{I}+i_M}\frac{\partial E_T}{\partial y}\frac{\partial y}{\partial v_n}$$

In these latter equations the first terms indicate the marginal unit costs of the services, and the remaining two the present value of the marginal *value* productivities of the services with respect to the two products. As in the case of simple production we therefore get the corollary to the maximum conditions that in order to get a maximum rate of return, the firm will employ each productive service until its marginal unit cost is equal to the present value of its marginal value productivity with respect to each one of the products, and it will employ capital funds until the marginal rate of return becomes equal to the marginal rate of interest. This condition holds true for any number of services and any number of products, and with the productive resources allocated in this way, no further gain can be obtained either by a substitution between the different products or by a substitution between the different services.[1]

With these maximum conditions once established, it is an easy task, at least in theory, to trace the effect of changes in the different production determining forces on the volume of production and the rate of return. As

---

[1] Compare the example of a building activity given by Marshall in his mathematical note XIV, (*Principles, op. cit.*, p. 848): "Thus he (the entrepreneur) will have distributed his resources between various uses in such a way that he would gain nothing by diverting any part of any agent of production — labour, raw material, the use of capital — nor his own labour and enterprise from one class of building to another: also he would gain nothing by substituting one agent for another in any branch of his enterprise, nor indeed by any increase or diminution of his use of any agent."

in the case of simple production we find that increased technical efficiency, decreased service prices, a decreased rate of interest and increased demand will all have a general increasing effect on the rate of return and, in so far as they affect the marginal costs and the marginal revenues, also on the volume of production. If, instead, the technical efficiency is lowered, the service prices or the rate of interest have gone up or the demand is diminished, the general effects will be the opposite. But, in contrast to simple production, we now have a joint output of two products, and the particular effect of the changes on these products may be different. If, for example, the increased demand refers to only one of the products, this product will increase in output, but, depending on the technical and demand relations between the products, the output of the other may remain constant or even decrease.[1] Other changes, such as changing service prices or a changing interest rate, may merely affect the two products in different degrees.

---

[1] Cf. Kreps, *op. cit.*, p. 442: "In the intermediate processes of the dye-stuffs industry, for example, there is a regular variation of processes with the ups and downs of business. In periods of rising prices, interactions are speeded up, with the penalty of increasing waste, but the reward of extra profits, due to getting the product on the market as quickly as possible. In periods of low prices attention is given to yields and to by-products."

CHAPTER VI

INTRODUCTION TO THE POLY-PERIODIC PRODUCTION THEORY.

Throughout the preceding pages, in the chapters both on simple and on joint production, we have been concerned with a production so arranged that one period's activity was entirely separate from the activities of preceding and subsequent periods. The inputs and outputs, the costs and revenues of one period were assumed to be determined exclusively by the conditions prevailing in that period, and to bear no relation to future and past inputs and outputs or costs and revenues. We had, in other words, what we have called a mono-periodic production. The assumptions on which our discussion was based were, however, highly artificial. In actual production the activity at any given time is generally closely interrelated both with the past and the future. The inputs or costs of one period are connected not only with the output or revenue of that period but with a series of future outputs or revenue; and, conversely, the output or revenue of one period is the result of the inputs and costs of a series of previous periods. In our earlier terminology, then, actual production is not mono- but poly-periodic.

THE NATURE OF POLY-PERIODIC PRODUCTION.

1. *Initial assumptions.* — The purpose of the present chapter is not to give a fully developed poly-periodic production theory, but merely to point out and discuss some features and problems which are characteristic of poly-

periodic production and which have therefore not been discussed before. To make our task simpler, let us select for our analysis a production process which is as similar as possible to the types of production with which we are already familiar. Let us again consider a single firm which buys and pays for its productive resources at the beginning of the periods and sells the output of each period at the period's end. The output consists only of one single commodity. As before, the production activity is financed partly from the firm's own capital and partly from borrowed funds, and the interest charges on these funds are paid at the end of every period. So far, the setting of our poly-periodic problems is exactly the same as for the earlier mono-periodic analysis. But here we shall assume that the productive process is so arranged that the input and cost of one period are related to the output and revenue not only of that period but also of the nearest following period, and that consequently the output and revenue of the latter period are the result of the input and cost both of its own and the nearest preceding period. This simple alteration in our assumptions will be sufficient in order to illustrate most of the features characteristic of the poly-periodic production.

2. *Durable and non-durable resources.* — In our mono-periodic analysis we assumed that productive resources bought at the beginning of a period yielded services for that period only. In fact, we never spoke of productive resources as such, but only of the service performed by the resources, and it was these services that constituted the input of the production process. We treated the services both as units of purchase and as units of input. When we now abandon the assumption of a single self-contained period and consider a production activity which is planned for two consecutive periods at a time, it will be convenient to speak of the productive resource as different from the services of the resource. Productive resources which yield services for more than one period will be referred to as *durable resources;* while resources of the mono-periodic type, i. e. resources whose services last for one

period only, will be classified as *non-durable*.[1] The existence of durable resources represents one of the characteristic features of poly-periodic production.

This distinction between durable and non-durable resources must not, of course, be confounded with the distinction between fixed and variable services. A productive service has been classified as fixed or variable, we remember, depending upon whether the cost of the service varies or remains unchanged with a variation in the quantity produced. The services of non-durable resources, we found, can belong to either class. Certain kinds of labour or raw-materials we definitely regard as variable services; while other kinds of labour, such as the work of foremen and executives, can best be classified as fixed services. Also the durable resources yield services which may be either variable or fixed. When a firm procures a patent right or a factory building which lasts throughout a series of periods, the costs of the patent or the factory may generally be regarded as fairly independent of the particular outputs in the different periods, and the services of these resources are consequently regarded as fixed. On the other hand, when the firm buys or contracts to buy a large quantity of raw materials which last for the production of several periods, and which, therefore, represents a durable resource, the cost of these raw materials will stand in a definite relationship to each one of the consecutive outputs and the services of the resource will be a variable service. Often these sharp distinctions are, of course, difficult to apply in any particular case.[2] Such activities as repair and upkeep of machinery, which affect the produc-

---

[1] While we distinguish between durable and non-durable resources with reference to their *future* services, we are not interested in the *past*. Whether a production resource, for example, is obtained direct from nature or is "produced" makes no difference in the entrepreneur's calculations.

[2] Compare the accounting literature on depreciation: e. g. H. Grossman, *Die Abschreibung als Kostenfaktor*, (Berlin, 1925) pp. 30 ff.; E. Schmalenbach, "Über Abschreibungen", *Zeitschrift für handelswissenschaftliche Forschung*, XXIII (1929), 193—212; *Ibid. Grundlagen der Selbstkostenrechnung und Preispolitik*. (Leipzig, 1930), pp. 154 ff. and J. B. Canning, "A Certain Erratic Tendency in Accountants' Income Procedure", *Econometrica* (1933) pp. 52—62.

tion of several periods, are partly determined by the volume of output and partly by other factors, such as the age of the machines.[1] As in our earlier study we shall, however, disregard these practical difficulties and assume that a distinction between the different classes of services can be made.

3. *The technical interdependence and the production function.* — Let us return to the simple case of poly-periodic production earlier described. We have assumed a production activity so constituted that the input of one period is related to the output both to that period and the period next following. The output of the latter period, conversely, is the result of the input of its own and the nearest preceding period. Thus, if we use the following notations

t_I and t_{II} .... for the two periods,

x_I and x_{II} .... for the products which are finished and sold at the end of these periods, and

$v_{I_1}, \ldots, v_{I_n}$ and

$v_{II_1}, \ldots, v_{II_n}$ for the inputs of variable services during the respective periods,

we have assumed that together with certain fixed services, the variable services $v_{I_1}, \ldots, v_{I_n}$ in the first period produce a joint output of product x_I and *intermediate products* which in the second period together with the variable

---

[1] A reference to Keynes' concept of "user cost" may be of interest at this point. This concept he defines as follows (*The General Theory of Employment, Interest and Money*, op. cit. pp. 66—67): "An entrepreneur's user cost is by definition equal to

$$A_1 + (G' - B') - G,$$

where A_1 is the amount of our entrepreneur's purchases from other entrepreneurs, G the actual value of his capital equipment at the end of the period, and G' the value it might have had at the end of the period if he had refrained from using it and had spent the optimum sum B' on its maintenence" ..... "If industry is completely integrated or if the entrepreneur has bought nothing from outside, so that $A_1 = 0$, the user cost is simply the equivalent of the current disinvestment involved in using the equipment ....".

It is this latter element $(G' - B') - G$ of the user cost that corresponds to the variable part of the services of the durable resources, referred to above, and which therefore represents a variable cost of the period's output.

services $v_{II_1}, \ldots, v_{II_n}$ and certain fixed services produce
product x_{II} (see fig. 17). The fixed and variable services
may have their origin either from durable or non-durable
resources.[1] So far, as in the first period we have a joint
production of one product that is sold in that period and
other intermediate products, later to be used in the pro-

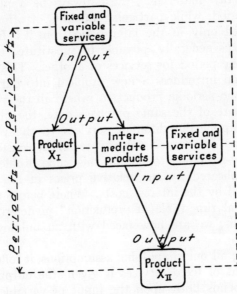

Fig. 17.

duction process, the present case of poly-periodic production shows a certain resemblance to the case of joint mono-
periodic production, except that the finished products
now have different selling dates. We may, indeed, define
poly-periodic production as *joint production in time*, although this joint production in actual life is generally of
a very complex character.

As has already been pointed out, we may expect that
the variable services in every period can to some extent

[1] Cf. A. Smithies, "The Austrian Theory of Capital in Relation to
Partial Equilibrium Theory," *Quarterly Journal of Economics*, L (1935/36),
p. 129: "..... if durable instruments are used, it is their services per
unit of time that appear as factors of production in the production function."

be substituted for one another. But since in the present case the output in one period is related to inputs of two consecutive periods, we may expect to find a substitution relation also between services of different dates. This service substitution may sometimes be limited by a certain technical rigidity, so that particular amounts of some services, such as "raw materials", must always be applied in the earlier period, while particular amounts of other services are applied only in the later period; but it is frequently, and perhaps generally, possible to substitute certain services of one period for services of another. This temporal substitution introduces a new problem into our analysis. Under mono-periodic production, where all the productive services were of the same purchase date, the question of when to apply the different services to the production process was determined only by technical considerations; under poly-periodic production, this same problem is further complicated by the relative prices in the different periods and by the interest costs. Where before there was a "technical time-table of production" predetermined for our analysis, we are now faced with an unknown to be solved.[1]

Granting all our simplifying assumptions, it follows that, if the input of fixed services is given, the output of one period depends both upon the input of variable services and upon the output of the other period. On analogy with the case of joint mono-periodic production, we may therefore write the products x_I and x_{II} as functions

(1a) $x_I = \varphi_{(x_I)} (v_{I_1}, \ldots, v_{I_n}, v_{II_1}, \ldots v_{II_n}, x_{II})$

and

(1b) $x_{II} = \varphi_{(x_{II})} (v_{I_1}, \ldots, v_{I_n}, v_{II_1}, \ldots v_{II_n}, x_I)$.

The partial derivatives of these functions give us, also here, the marginal productivities of the services with res-

---

[1] Compare the discussions of "speeds of turnover" and "delay periods" of the productive factors by Leontief and Smithies. (W. Leontief, "Interest on Capital and Distribution: A problem in the theory of marginal productivity," *Quarterly Journal of Economics*, XLIX (1934/35) p. 151, and Smithies, *op. cit.*, pp. 124 ff.)

pect to the two products[1] and the substitution relation between these products.[2] There are other similarities between our present poly-periodic and joint mono-periodic productions. For instance, we may notice again that an infinitesimal increase of the variable services produces an increase of x_I, when x_{II} is constant, or of x_{II}, when x_I is constant, which is equal to the sum of the marginal products of the services in respect to x_I and x_{II} respectively

$$(2a) \quad dx_I = \frac{\partial x_I}{\partial v_{I_1}} dv_{I_1} + \ldots + \frac{\partial x_I}{\partial v_{IIn}} dv_{IIn} \quad (x_{II} = \text{constant})$$

and

$$(2b) \quad dx_{II} = \frac{\partial x_{II}}{\partial v_{I_1}} dv_{I_1} + \ldots + \frac{\partial x_{II}}{\partial v_{IIn}} dv_{IIn} \quad (x_I = \text{constant}).$$

The difference is that in poly-periodic production the marginal products relate to services of two different dates. As in the case of joint production, the technical relationships between x_I and x_{II} may be complementary, competing or independent, but this relationship can be measured only in terms of marginal costs.

THE POLY-PERIODIC EXPANSION PATH.

In mono-period production we distinguished between two classes of production costs: the costs of productive services and the interest costs. But, since all productive services entering into a product were bought at the same date, the interest costs were simply proportional to the service costs and had but little influence on the cost relations of production. The expansion path, for example, was determined solely by the service costs, irrespective of the height of the rate of interest. Under poly-periodic assumptions the situation is quite different. Since here the pro-

---

[1] Compare J. R. Hicks, "Wages and Interest: The Dynamic Problem," *Economic Journal*, XLV (1935), p. 461, n. 1: ".... the labour of any period has as many marginal products as there are periods under consideration, for it will be possible, by employing extra labour at any particular date, to increase output at any other period we choose."

[2] Compare Hart, *op. cit.* pp. 43 ff.

ductive services for a given output are assumed to be bought at different dates, not only the service prices but also the interest costs will affect the expansion path chosen.

1. *The price interdependence.* — As long as we were considering a single self-contained time period, we could assume that the prices paid for productive services were determined exclusively by the amounts of the services bought at a particular time. The same held true with regard to the interest rate and the amount of borrowed or invested capital funds. Under our present assumptions, on the other hand, we must consider the service prices and the interest rate of one period as determined by earlier and later purchases, borrowing or investments as well.

This price interdependence between the different periods depends partly on the existence of durable resources and partly on the actions of the sellers. An increased purchase of a service and a higher price in an early period may, for instance, attract a certain supply of the service which otherwise would not have appeared until later periods, and by so doing cause a rise in future prices. Or, if the sellers assume that the increased demand of the firm is permanent, the effect may be reversed. Attracted by higher wages in the first periods, new labourers may move to the locality, to remain there even if the firm's labour demand slackens later. Similarly, a decreased purchase and a lower price for a service in an early period may postpone the marketing of a part of the supply to later periods, thereby causing lower future prices, or a decrease in purchases may permanently diminish the service supply and so cause future prices to go up. In an analogous way, the firm's demand for a service in a later period, if announced in advance or anticipated by the sellers of the service, may influence the service prices also in an earlier period.

With reference to the interest rate the price interdependence between the different periods is still more complex. The rate of interest that the firm in a certain period has to pay for its borrowed funds, or gets on its outside investments, is influenced not only by the amounts of borrowing and investment in that and neighbouring periods, but also by the length of time over which the borrowing or investment is made and by the securities given. A firm may, for example, obtain a lower interest rate if it borrows on short terms, or if it invests the funds in a particular way, for instance in factory buildings instead of in office machinery. In our present analysis, which after all is only the outline of a poly-periodic production theory, we shall, however, disregard all these complexities, and simply assume that the interest rate both for borrowing and lending in every particular period is determined solely by the amounts borrowed or invested in that period. By making such an assumption we shall pass over many interesting details of the poly-periodic theory in order that the main relationships which we must consider may gain in lucidity.

2. *The expansion path.* — What influence has now this price interdependence on the determination of the poly-periodic expansion path? For the sake of convenience let us approach the problem as it appears at the beginning of the first period, that is, at the time when the whole process is planned. The prices of a certain service, v_k, in the two periods we write

$$q_{Ik} = q_{Ik}(v_{Ik}, v_{IIk}) \quad \text{and} \quad q_{IIk} = q_{IIk}(v_{Ik}, v_{IIk}).$$

If, at the substitution margin, the service in the first period is changed by one unit, this change will affect the cost of the service not only in that but also in the second period, and *vice versa.* In order to find the marginal unit cost of the service we have, therefore, to consider the effect of the change on the total cost of the service in both periods, inclusive of interest cost. This total cost we write

$$C_{v_k} = q_{Ik} v_{Ik} + \frac{1}{1 + i_I} q_{IIk} v_{IIk}$$

where i_I is the average interest rate of the first period. The partial derivatives of this cost with respect to v_{Ik} and

v_{IIk} give us the marginal unit costs of the service in the two periods

$$c_{v_{Ik}} = \frac{\partial C_{v_k}}{\partial v_{Ik}} = \left[q_{Ik} + v_{Ik} \frac{\partial q_{Ik}}{\partial v_{Ik}} \right] + \frac{1}{1 + i_{M_I}} v_{IIk} \frac{\partial q_{IIk}}{\partial v_{Ik}}$$

and

$$c_{v_{IIk}} = \frac{\partial C_{v_k}}{\partial v_{IIk}} = v_{Ik} \frac{\partial q_{Ik}}{\partial v_{IIk}} + \frac{1}{1 + i_{M_I}} \left[q_{IIk} + v_{IIk} \frac{\partial q_{IIk}}{\partial v_{IIk}} \right]$$

where i_{M_I} represents the marginal rate of interest which, according to our assumptions, is determined in the same way as in our earlier mono-periodic analysis. The cost-productivity ratios which represent the quotient between the marginal unit costs of the services and their marginal productivities with respect to the different products, we consequently write

$$x_I c_{v_{Ik}} = \frac{\dfrac{\partial C_{v_k}}{\partial v_{Ik}}}{\dfrac{\partial x_I}{\partial v_{Ik}}}, \qquad x_{II} c_{v_{Ik}} = \frac{\dfrac{\partial C_{v_k}}{\partial v_{Ik}}}{\dfrac{\partial x_{II}}{\partial v_{Ik}}}, \qquad x_I c_{v_{IIk}} = \frac{\dfrac{\partial C_{v_k}}{\partial v_{IIk}}}{\dfrac{\partial x_I}{\partial v_{IIk}}}$$

and

$$x_{II} c_{v_{IIk}} = \frac{\dfrac{\partial C_{v_k}}{\partial v_{IIk}}}{\dfrac{\partial x_{II}}{\partial v_{IIk}}}.$$

On analogy with the case of joint mono-periodic production, the minimum cost combination for a given output is obtained when the marginal unit costs of the different services are proportional to the marginal productivities of the services with respect to each one of the consecutive products, or, which amounts to the same thing, when the cost-productivity ratios with respect to every product are equal

$$\frac{\partial C_{v_1}}{\partial v_{I_1}} : \cdots : \frac{\partial C_{v_n}}{\partial v_{II_n}} = \frac{\partial x_I}{\partial v_{I_1}} : \cdots : \frac{\partial x_I}{\partial v_{II_n}} = \frac{\partial x_{II}}{\partial v_{I_1}} : \cdots : \frac{\partial x}{\partial v_{II_n}}$$

(3) or

$$\frac{\dfrac{\partial C_{v_1}}{\partial v_{I_1}}}{\dfrac{\partial x_I}{\partial v_{I_1}}} = \ldots = \frac{\dfrac{\partial C_{v_n}}{\partial v_{IIn}}}{\dfrac{\partial x_I}{\partial v_{IIn}}} \quad \text{and} \quad \frac{\dfrac{\partial C_{v_1}}{\partial v_{I_1}}}{\dfrac{\partial x_{II}}{\partial v_{I_1}}} = \ = \frac{\dfrac{\partial C_{v_n}}{\partial v_{IIn}}}{\dfrac{\partial x_{II}}{\partial v_{IIn}}}$$

But, as in the case of joint production described above, the relative magnitudes of the cost productivity ratios are still to be determined.[1]

If we assume that there is no price interdependence between the periods, the cost-productivity ratios become

$$\frac{q_{1k}(1 + \lambda_{Ik})}{\dfrac{\partial x_I}{\partial v_{I_1}}} = \ldots = \frac{1}{1 + i_{M_I}} \frac{q_{IIn}(1 + \lambda_{IIn})}{\dfrac{\partial x_I}{\partial v_{IIn}}}$$

and

$$\frac{q_{I_1}(1 + \lambda_{I_1})}{\dfrac{\partial x_{II}}{\partial v_{I_1}}} = \ldots = \frac{1}{1 + i_{M_I}} \frac{q_{IIn}(1 + \lambda_{IIn})}{\dfrac{\partial x_{II}}{\partial v_{IIn}}}$$

where the λ's are the simple price flexibilities of the services in the respective periods. It thus becomes clear that when productive services which enter into the same product are bought in *the same* period, these services will be substituted for one another until their marginal productivities with respect to that product become proportional to the service prices multiplied by one plus the price flexibilities, a condition which fully conforms to the earlier mono-periodic conditions. It is also clear that when a durable resource yields variable services which in consecutive periods enter into the production of *the same* product, these services will be so distributed between the

---

[1] Since for different producers, even if they are working in the same locality,
   (1) the age and efficiency of the "fixed" technical equipment,
   (2) the supply conditions of productive services, and
   (3) the supply conditions of capital funds are generally different, it follows that the expansion paths chosen are also different. So, for example, Myrdal observes that the service combinations selected by a firm which borrows funds are generally different from those selected by a firm which invests only its own capital. (Cf. *Prisbildningsproblemet och föränderligheten, op. cit.*, p. 219.)

periods that their marginal productivities are the same. Thus, if v_{Ik} and v_{IIk} are the services of a durable resource, bought at the beginning of the first period, these services will be substituted for one another until

$$\frac{\partial x_I}{\partial v_{Ik}} = \frac{\partial x_I}{\partial v_{IIk}} \quad \text{and} \quad \frac{\partial x_{II}}{\partial v_{Ik}} = \frac{\partial x_{II}}{\partial v_{IIk}}.$$

This relation assumes, however, that there exists no cost for the upkeep or storage of the resources. On the other hand, if a productive service which has entered into the production of the same product throughout two periods is bought successively in both periods, it will be so distributed between the periods that its marginal productivity in the earlier period exceeds its marginal productivity in the later period by an amount which corresponds to the interest costs. If, for example, the service v_k has the same price in both periods, it will be employed in such a way that

$$\frac{\dfrac{\partial x_I}{\partial v_{Ik}}}{\dfrac{\partial x_I}{\partial v_{IIk}}} = \frac{\dfrac{\partial x_{II}}{\partial v_{Ik}}}{\dfrac{\partial x_{II}}{\partial v_{IIk}}} = 1 + i_{M_I}.$$

Furthermore, if a durable resource yields services which enter into the production of a series of consecutive outputs, the distribution of these services over the different periods will also be influenced by the interest costs. Thus, if all other production determining forces remain unchanged, a fall in the interest cost will stimulate a slower and a rise in the interest cost a more rapid exhaustion of the durable resource.[1]

COSTS, REVENUES AND OUTPUT.

1. *Joint costs in time.* — The interdependence between different periods which is characteristic of poly-

[1] These conclusions, we may observe, are in full harmony with the Wicksellean theory of capital. [Cf. Knut Wicksell, *Über Wert, Kapital und Rente* (Jena, 1893) pp. 95 ff. and *Lectures on Political Economy*, (Engl. transl., New York, 1934), vol. i, pp. 172 ff.]

periodic production may be found also in the relationship between costs and output. The causes of this temporal cost interdependence are already familiar. We have assumed a production activity so arranged that the input of productive services in one period and consequently also the cost of these services are related to the output of two different periods. Furthermore, the price interdependence existing between different dates causes the cost of the productive services bought in one period to be influenced by service purchases in other periods, and finally, the existence of durable productive resources, which, although bought in one period, yield their services also in other periods, gives rise to costs which are related to several outputs. Because of these interrelating elements there is no possibility of allocating the poly-periodic costs to the different products except at the substitution margin. As in the case of mono-periodic joint production, we must write the total cost of the production activity, C, which here also includes interest costs, as a function of the two outputs x_I and x_{II}

$$C = C\ (x_I,\ x_{II}).$$

Since in the present case the products are of different selling dates, we may speak of *joint costs in time*.[1]

The partial derivatives of the cost function with respect to the two consecutive products give us the marginal cost of the products which are equal to the cost-productivity ratios of the different services with respect to the two products[2]

---

[1] It is interesting to notice that the first example of joint production which, as far as I know, was ever given in economic literature represents a case of "joint production in time". I refer to Longfield's passage about crop rotation. Compare *Lectures on Political Economy* (Dublin, 1834), p. 246: "The business of farming is .... still more complicated. This complexity arises from the necessity of rotation of crops. .... As an illustration, let us consider what would be the effects of the general introduction of turnip husbandry into a country where it was previously unknown. The first effect would be to diminish the cost of production of sheep — the animal fed on that root — and of wheat, as the crop next in rotation ...."

[2] The proof of this proposition, which is similar to the proof given in Chapter V, p. 89 n. 1, is here omitted.

$$(4) \quad \begin{cases} \dfrac{\partial C}{\partial x_{\mathrm{I}}} = x_{\mathrm{I}} c_{v_{\mathrm{I}_1}} = \ldots = x_{\mathrm{I}} c_{v_{\mathrm{II}_n}} \\ \text{and} \\ \dfrac{\partial C}{\partial x_{\mathrm{II}}} = x_{\mathrm{II}} c_{v_{\mathrm{I}_1}} = \ldots = x_{\mathrm{II}} c_{v_{\mathrm{II}_n}}. \end{cases}$$

The properties of the marginal costs are determined by the second derivatives $\dfrac{\partial^2 C}{\partial x_{\mathrm{I}}{}^2}$ and $\dfrac{\partial^2 C}{\partial x_{\mathrm{II}}{}^2}$ and the mixed derivative $\dfrac{\partial^2 C}{\partial x_{\mathrm{I}} \partial x_{\mathrm{II}}}$, and in the latter derivative we find, once more, a criterion for the technical interdependence between the products. Thus, when the service prices are constant, a positive, negative, or zero value of the derivative $\dfrac{\partial^2 C}{\partial x_{\mathrm{I}} \partial x_{\mathrm{II}}}$ indicates that the products x_{I} and x_{II} are, respectively, technically complementary, competing or independent.

Before we leave the discussion of the poly-periodic costs a few words should be said with regard to the cost of the durable resources. By definition, the durable resources yield services over a series of consecutive periods. At first we shall assume that the number of these periods is given, that is, that raw materials are always bought to meet the needs of a fixed number of periods, that machines are built to last a given time etc. The cost of the durable resources consequently represents a joint cost for the output of a given number of periods. If the services yielded by the resources are fixed services, such as the services of a patent right; or of a machine which quickly becomes obsolete or for which the "wear and tear" depends on its age only and not on the amount of use it has given,[1] this joint cost will be independent of the quantities of output produced. There will exist no problem of how to distribute the services as between the different periods,

---

[1] We may notice that the effects of obsolecence and "wear and tear" on the firm's costs are identical, except that the effect of "wear and tear" is generally easier to calculate.

and no possibility of allocating the cost over the different outputs, not even at the production margin. On the other hand, if the services of the durable resources are variable services, such as the services of raw materials bought for a series of subsequent periods, the cost of the resources will depend on the amount of the services rendered, and thus also on the output produced in the different periods. Even then, however, the costs of the resources cannot be distributed over the different outputs, except at the production margin.

If we abandon the assumption of a fixed durability and assume that the productive resources can be bought to last for a variable number of periods, we find a definite relationship between the cost of the resources and their durability. Thus, if a resource is bought to last a longer time than before, its initial cost and its cost for repair and upkeep will increase, but generally to a lesser degree than its durability. The lower initial cost, measured per output period, will, however, at least partially be balanced by higher interest costs. Other things being equal, therefore, the choice of the most profitable durability and dates of replacements of the durable productive resources will depend on the interest rates anticipated in the different periods.[1]

2. *The interdependence of demand and the production revenue.* — As before, we shall assume that the entrepreneur has a definite expectation pattern with regard to the demand of the firm's output in the different periods. But, whereas in our mono-periodic analysis we assumed the pattern to be so constituted that the anticipated price in one period was determined by the output of that period only, we must now consider a price interdependence of the outputs in different periods similar to the price interdependence of the productive services earlier discussed. An increased output of an earlier period and a correspond-

[1] Compare G. Åkerman, *Realkapital und Kapitalzins*, vols. I and II (Stockholm, 1923 and 1924), and K. Wicksell, Realkapital och kapital-ränta, *Ekonomisk Tidskrift*, XXV (1923) pp. 145—180, Engl. transl. *Lectures, op. cit.*, vol. I pp. 258—299. See also E. Schneider, "Das Zeit-moment in der Theorie der Produktion," *Jahrbücher für Nationalökonomie und Statistik*, Band 143 (1936), pp. 45—67.

ingly lower price, for example, may attract some demand which otherwise would have appeared only in later periods, or it may "spoil the market" in these periods, and thereby have a decreasing effect on future demand. Or the increased output and decreased price may cause new types of demand to develop which will carry over to some extent if the price is raised in the future, or, cause competitors to leave the market permanently. Examples of the latter situation may be found in railroads which by offering low rates during certain years build up a permanent demand for freight service. Correspondingly, an increased output and decreased price for a later period announced in advance or anticipated by the buyers may have an increasing or decreasing effect on the demand also of earlier periods.

Also with respect to the demand conditions the poly-periodic production consequently shows many similarities to mono-periodic joint production. Because of the interdependence of demand between different periods, in the particular case here assumed the prices of the two consecutive products, p_I and p_{II}, become functions of two variables, x_I and x_{II},

$$p_I = p_I (x_I, x_{II}) \text{ and } p_{II} = p_{II} (x_I, x_{II})$$

and the same holds true of the total revenue, E,

$$E = E (x_I, x_{II}).$$

The partial derivatives of the revenue function with respect to the two products, once more, give us the marginal revenues of the products. To these relationships we shall return later.

The Poly-Periodic Maximization Problem.

The interdependence between different time periods which is the specific feature of the poly-periodic production affects also the maximization problem. The result of a present period's production is related to the activities of past periods through durable productive resources and intermediate products which exist at the beginning of the period, and to the activities of future periods because these activities are partly the outcome of present inputs and costs. We shall first consider the influence of durable resources and intermediate products.

1. *The valuation of the firm's investments.* — In the simple case of poly-periodic production under consideration, let us assume that the firm's own capital is exclusively invested in durable productive resources inherited from a previous period. At the beginning of period t_I, consequently, the firm has no liquid funds, and the purchases of productive services in the period have to be financed through outside borrowing. This assumption will greatly simplify our argument without affecting its main result. Let us, for the time being, also assume that the rates of interest for borrowing and for lending are equal to each other and constant inside every separate period, an assumption which we shall modify later.

The value of the firm's investments in durable resources at the beginning of period t_I can be determined in either of two different ways: by a consideration of the selling prices of the resources at that date, or of their anticipated future net returns if used in the firm's production. The value obtained by the first method we shall refer to as the *realization value*, K_R, the value obtained by the second method as the *use value*, K_U, of the investments.[1] If the durable resources consist of relatively standardized products which have a general market, these two values will tend to be equal. Otherwise the use value of the resource will generally exceed the realization value. Should the realization value be the higher, the firm would sell its productive resources and cease to continue its production.

If the revenues anticipated at the end of the two periods are denoted by E_I and E_{II}, the anticipated outlays for productive services at the beginning of the periods by C_I and C_{II}, and the interest rates by i_I and i_{II}, the use

---

[1] This concept of use value must not be confused with Keynes' concept of "user cost", which is something entirely different. See above p. 106 n. 1.

value of the firm's investments at the beginning of period t_I becomes

$$(5) \quad K_U = \frac{E_I}{(1 + i_I)} + \frac{E_{II}}{(1 + i_I)(1 + i_{II})} - C_I - \frac{C_{II}}{(1 + i_I)}.$$

The first two terms in this sum represent the discounted value of the total revenue

$$E = E(x_I, x_{II})$$

and the last two terms the discounted value of the total costs

$$C = C(x_I, x_{II})$$

at the beginning of the period. Thus the use value of the firm's investments in durable resources at a given date is equal to the difference between the discounted total revenue and discounted total costs at that date.

2. *The net return and the rate of return.* — Let us now shift our attention to the end of period t_I, and examine the factors which determine the *net return* of the first period. The net return of a period we have defined as the difference between the total revenue and the total costs for the period, inclusive of interest costs on borrowed funds. In the present case, however, the costs of period t_I are related not only to the revenue of t_I, as in mono-periodic production, but also to the costs and revenue of the second period. The discounted values of these elements must be included in the net return. Furthermore, while in the mono-periodic case the firm's capital funds were subtracted from the revenue as a part of the costs of productive services, these funds now represent durable resources, and are, therefore, not included in the costs of the period. To get a correct value of the net return in the period the realization value of the durable resources must be entered as a minus item in the calculations. Using the same symbols as before, we therefore write the net return of period t_I

$$(6) \quad R_I = E_I + \frac{E_{II}}{(1 + i_{II})} - C_I(1 + i_I) - C_{II} - K_R$$

where K_R represents the realization value of the durable resources. If we express the net return thus obtained as a rate on the realization value of the firm's investments we get the *rate of return* in the period

$$r_\mathrm{I} = \frac{R_\mathrm{I}}{K_R}.$$

A comparison between equations (5) and (6) shows that the net return of period t_I may be written

(6a) $$R_\mathrm{I} = K_U \left(1 + i_\mathrm{I}\right) - K_R.$$

Since the realization value of the firm's investments is externally determined, it therefore follows that under our present assumptions of constant interest rates which are equal for borrowing and lending, the maximum conditions must be the same irrespective of whether we maximize the rate of return, the net return or the use value of the firm's investments. We may choose anyone of the three.

In the determination of the net return we have referred to the firm's investments in durable resources at their realization value because this value represents a pre-determined quantity. If in equation (6a) we instead introduce the use value of the investments, the net return simply becomes equal to the interest on the use value in the period

$$R_\mathrm{I} = K_U i_\mathrm{I}.$$

The net return here merely signifies the appreciation of the firm's capital during the period due to the fact that future returns of the capital have come nearer. This is the idea which underlies Lindahl's concept of "income as interest".[1]

---

[1] Cf. E. Lindahl, "The Concept of Income", *Economic Essays in Honour of Gustav Cassel*, (London, 1933), p. 400: Interest as income ... "may be taken as referring to the continuous *appreciation* of capital goods owing to the time-factor, that is to say, the current interest on the capital value which the goods represent." ..... "Capital value must again be the starting point for the estimation of income as interest, that is to say, as the appreciation which arises when the discounted future services come nearer and nearer — an increase in value which for a given period forward can be regarded as the product of the capital value and the rate of interest applying to the period."

3. *The maximum conditions.* — To determine the most profitable production we have to differentiate the net return, the rate of return or the use value of the firm's investments partially with respect to the two consecutive outputs, and set these partial derivatives equal to zero. If we choose the use value of the investments as given in equation (5), we get

$$\frac{\partial K_U}{\partial x_I} = \frac{1}{(1+i_I)}\left[\frac{\partial E_I}{\partial x_I} + \frac{1}{(1+i_{II})}\frac{\partial E_{II}}{\partial x_I}\right] - \frac{\partial C_I}{\partial x_I} - \frac{1}{(1+i_I)}\frac{\partial C_{II}}{\partial x_I} = 0$$

and

$$\frac{\partial K_U}{\partial x_{II}} = \frac{1}{(1+i_I)}\left[\frac{\partial E_I}{\partial x_{II}} + \frac{1}{(1+i_{II})}\frac{\partial E_{II}}{\partial x_{II}}\right] - \frac{\partial C_I}{\partial x_{II}} - \frac{1}{(1+i_I)}\frac{\partial C_{II}}{\partial x_{II}} = 0$$

The first two terms in these equations represent the discounted values of the marginal revenues and the last two terms the discounted values of the marginal costs at the beginning of the first period. Again, we therefore have as a maximum condition that the marginal revenues must be equal to the marginal costs

$$\frac{\partial E}{\partial x_I} = \frac{\partial C}{\partial x_I} \quad \text{and} \quad \frac{\partial E}{\partial x_{II}} = \frac{\partial C}{\partial x_{II}}$$

although, in the present case, it is the properly discounted values of these elements that must be equal. Furthermore, since the marginal costs of the two consecutive products are equal to the cost-productivity ratios of the different services with respect to the products, we have

$$\frac{\frac{\partial C_{v_1}}{\partial v_{I_1}}}{\frac{\partial x_I}{\partial v_{I_1}}} = \ldots = \frac{\frac{\partial C_{v_n}}{\partial v_{IIn}}}{\frac{\partial x_I}{\partial v_{IIn}}} = \frac{\partial E}{\partial x_I} \quad \text{and} \quad \frac{\frac{\partial C_{v_1}}{\partial v_{I_1}}}{\frac{\partial x_{II}}{\partial v_{I_1}}} = \ldots = \frac{\frac{\partial C_{v_n}}{\partial v_{IIn}}}{\frac{\partial x_{II}}{\partial v_{IIn}}} = \frac{\partial E}{\partial x_{II}}$$

or, if we write the equations in another way,

$$\frac{\partial C_{v_1}}{\partial v_{I_1}} = \frac{\partial E}{\partial x_I} \cdot \frac{\partial x_I}{\partial v_{I_1}} = \frac{\partial E}{\partial x_{II}} \frac{\partial x_{II}}{\partial v_{I_1}}$$

$$\frac{\partial C_{v_2}}{\partial v_{I_2}} = \frac{\partial E}{\partial x_I} \cdot \frac{\partial x_I}{\partial v_{I_2}} = \frac{\partial E}{\partial x_{II}} \frac{\partial x_{II}}{\partial v_{I_2}}$$

$$\cdots\cdots\cdots\cdots\cdots\cdots$$

$$\cdots\cdots\cdots\cdots\cdots\cdots$$

$$\frac{\partial C_{vn}}{\partial v_{IIn}} = \frac{\partial E}{\partial x_I} \cdot \frac{\partial x_I}{\partial v_{IIn}} = \frac{\partial E}{\partial x_{II}} \frac{\partial x_{II}}{\partial v_{IIn}}$$

The elements on the left side in these latter equations indicate the marginal unit costs of the productive services at the beginning of the first period, and the elements on the right side the marginal value productivities of the services with respect to the successive products discounted back to the same date. As in the case of joint mono-periodic production we therefore have as a corollary to the maximum conditions that, in order to get a maximum use value on the firm's investments, a maximum net return or a maximum rate of return, the firm will employ each productive service until its marginal unit cost is equal to its discounted marginal value productivity with respect to each product. This condition holds true for the services of both durable and non-durable resources, and for all types of production, irrespective of whether the technical and price interdependence between the periods is simple or complex, or of whether the outputs of the different periods are composed of one or several commodities.

Changes in the production determining forces will generally have the same effect on a poly-periodic production as on a joint mono-periodic production of the type earlier discussed. An increase in the product prices, for example, or a decrease in the prices of the variable services or the interest rates will cause the scale of production to expand and the rate of return to rise. But there are other phenomena which are peculiar to the poly-periodic production. With some of these, such as the technical interdependence and the price interdependence between the different periods, we are already familiar. We have, for instance, also observed that a change in the interest rate influences not only the volume of production, as in the mono-periodic case, but also the selection of durable productive resources and the choice of service combinations. An increased interest rate stimulates a substitution of services of later periods for services of earlier periods, and a diminution of the durability of the durable resources. A decreased interest rate has the opposite effect.

Another characteristic feature of the poly-periodic relationships is that a given change in the production determining forces will have a different effect on the scale and methods of production depending on when the change takes place. While, for example, an anticipated temporary change in the demand for finished products or in the supply of productive services in the second period will influence the selection of durable resources and the production of intermediate products in the preceding period also, a corresponding change of the demand or service supply in the first period will have no such effect. So long as there exist old durable resources, such as buildings and machinery, the net return is influenced to a rather limited degree by changes in the methods and volume of production. More important changes require a renewal of the durable productive resources, a process which can often take place only step by step over a long period of time, and which therefore has to be planned in advance.[1]

4. *The influence of variable interest rates.* — The maximum conditions so far developed rest on the assumption of a constant interest rate in every separate period. If we leave this assumption and again regard the interest rates as functions of the amounts of borrowing and investment, the results of our analysis will be slightly changed. With a series of different borrowing and investment opportunities at his disposal, the entrepreneur will shift his capital in such a way that the marginal rates of inter-

[1] For a discussion of these more "dynamic" production relations compare Myrdal, *Prisbildningsproblemet och föränderligheten*, op. cit. Ch. V, and E. Lindahl, "Prisbildningsproblemets uppläggning ur kapitalteoretisk synpunkt", *Ekonomisk Tidskrift*, XXXI (1929), pp. 31—81.

est on borrowing and lending in every period become the same, and expand his current production until the marginal revenue and marginal costs, discounted with the marginal interest rates, are equal. Thus, the maximum conditions are the same as in the case of constant interest rates, except that here it is the marginal rates of interest that enter into the calculations. But this similarity holds true with regard to the marginal relationships only. Although the marginal interest rates must be the same on borrowing and lending, the average rates are generally different both between various borrowing and investment opportunities and as compared with the entrepreneur's own preference scale of future incomes. Whether under these conditions such concepts as net revenue [equation (6)] and use value of the firm's investments [equation (5)] have any definite meaning seems highly questionable. Its actual determination would, at least, be extremely difficult.

SOME FURTHER PROBLEMS OF THE PURE THEORY OF PRODUCTION.

With these observations about the influence on the poly-periodic production of variable interest rates our study has come to an end. But before we conclude the essay let us once more repeat the general assumptions on which the analysis has been based. At the same time, we may also point out some further problems of the pure theory of production which still await solution. Throughout the essay we have been concerned with the production of the single business firm, and we have analysed the different production problems from the viewpoint of the individual firm. Such conditions as those determining the supply of productive services and capital funds or the demand of the firm's output, we have simply assumed as given, and we have disregarded the possibility for the firm to influence these conditions by means of sales promotion or similar activities We have further assumed that there exists no price discrimination whatsoever, and no price interdependence between different dates with regard to capital funds.

A modification of the analysis to include the problems of price discrimination need not raise any serious theoretical difficulties, and the same probably holds true also for the problems of temporal interdependence with respect to the interest rates. The whole question of variable interest rates and their influence on the poly-periodic production requires, however, a much more thorough analysis than the introductory observations made here.

Another task is to relate the present theory of the individual firm to the theories of monopolistic or imperfect competition, and to examine the mutual interdependence between the productive activity of the firm and the different market conditions. The relationship between sales promotion and demand for finished products has recently been discussed in the literature, but so far the analysis has primarily been made under mono-periodic assumptions. A more extensive examination of such problems as how the existence of durable productive resources affects the sales promotion policy of the firm during the different phases of the business cycle, or how the sales promotion in one period affects the demand of the firm's output in other periods still remains to be undertaken. And there are many other poly-periodic problems both with regard to the firm's selling activity and its bidding in the service and capital markets which ought to be discussed. Despite the facts that the analysis rests on such simplifying assumptions and that so many interesting and important relationships have necessarily been omitted from consideration, this study represents, I hope, a frame-work for the pure theory of production which further researches will modify and fill out but not substantially change.

SELECTED BIBLIOGRAPHY.

Books.

ÅKERMAN, G. *Realkapital und Kapitalzins*. Vol. I and II. Stockholm: Centraltryckeriet, 1923 and 1924.

AMOROSO, L. *Lezioni di Economia Matematica*. Bologna: Nicola Zanichelli, 1921.

COURNOT, AUGUSTIN. *Researches into the Mathematical Principles of the Theory of Wealth*, (Bacon's transl.) 2nd ed. New York: Macmillan Co., 1929.

FANNO, MARCO. *Contributio alla teoria dell'offerta a costi congiunti*. Roma: Athenæum, 1914.

FISHER, IRVING. *The Nature of Capital and Income*. New York: Macmillan Co., 1906.

—, *The Theory of Interest*. New York: Macmillan Co., 1930.

KNIGHT, F. H. *Risk, Uncertainty and Profit*. Boston and New York: Houghton Mifflin Co., 1921.

MARSHALL, A. *Principles of Economics*. 8th ed. London: Macmillan and Co., Limited, 1920.

MOORE, H. L. *Synthetic Economics*, New York: Macmillan Co., 1929.

MYRDAL, G. *Prisbildningsproblemet och föränderligheten*. Uppsala: Almqvist och Wiksell, 1927.

PARETO, VILFREDO. *Manuel d'économie politique*. 2e éd. Paris: Marcel Giard, 1927.

SCHNEIDER, E. *Theorie der Produktion*. Wien: Julius Springer, 1934.

SCHMALENBACH, EUGEN. *Grundlagen der Selbstkostenrechnung und Preispolitik*, 5. Aufl. Leipzig: Gloeckner, 1930.

STACKELBERG, H. V. *Grundlagen einer reinen Kostentheorie*. Wien: Julius Springer, 1932.

WICKSELL, KNUT. *Über Wert, Kapital und Rente*. Jena: Gustav Fischer, 1893.

—, *Lectures on Political Economy*. Vol. I. New York: Macmillan Co., 1934.

Articles.

AMOROSO, L. "La curva statica di offerta", *Giornale degli Economisti*, LXX, 1930, pp. 1—26.

EDGEWORTH, F. Y. "The Laws of Increasing and Diminishing Returns," *Papers Relating to Political Economy*, Vol. I. London: Macmillan and Co., Limited, 1925, pp. 61—99.

—, "The Pure Theory of Monopoly", *Papers Relating to Political Economy*, Vol. I. London: Macmillan and Co., Limited, 1925, pp. 111—142.

128

HICKS, J. R. "Wages and Interest: The Dynamic Problem", *Economic Journal*, XLV (1935) pp. 456—468.

JOHNSON, W. E. "The Pure Theory of Utility Curves," *Economic Journal*, XXIII (1913), pp. 483—513.

LINDAHL, ERIK. "Prisbildningsproblemets uppläggning från kapitalteoretisk synpunkt," *Ekonomisk Tidskrift*, XXXI. (1929), pp. 31—81.

MYRDAL, G. "Der Gleichgewichtsbegriff als Instrument der geldtheoretischen Analyse." *Beiträge zur Geldtheorie.* (F. A. Hayek ed.) Wien: Julius Springer, 1933.

SCHULTZ, H. "Marginal Productivity and the General Pricing Process," *Journal of Political Economy*, XXXVII (1929), pp. 505—551.

SMITHIES, A. "The Austrian Theory of Capital in Relation to Partial Equilibrium Theory," *Quarterly Journal of Economics*, L (1935/36). pp. 117—150.

VINER, J. "Cost Curves and Supply Curves," *Zeitschrift für Nationalökonomie*, III (1931), pp. 23—46.

WICKSELL, KNUT. "Realkapital och kapitalränta," *Ekonomisk Tidskrift*, XXV (1923), pp. 145—180.

Unpublished Material.

FRISCH, R. "Tekniske og økonomiske produktivitetslover". Mimeographed lectures, University of Oslo.

HART, A. G. "Anticipations, Business Planning and the Cycle. An essay in the theory of economic disequilibrium." Doctor's dissertation, Dept. of Economics, University of Chicago, 1936.

MARSCHAK, J. "On Investments." The academic copying office, Oxford, 1935, (mimeographed).

OHLIN, BERTIL. "Omkostnadsanalys och prispolitik." Mimeographed lectures, Stockholm, 1934.